FATIH AKAY

2100

Exploring the World of 2100

To the dreamers and visionaries,
This book is dedicated to those who dare to look beyond the present and imagine
a future brimming with possibilities. It is for the dreamers who believe in the
transformative power of human ingenuity and the boundless potential of
scientific progress.

"The future belongs to those who believe in the beauty of their dreams."

– Eleanor Roosevelt

Contents

Foreword   iii
Preface   v
Acknowledgement   vii

I   The Dawn of a New Era

1   Prologue: A Glimpse into the Future   3
2   Shaping the Path: Socioeconomic Transformations   6

II   Technological Frontiers

3   Innovations that Redefine Humanity   21
4   Artificial Intelligence in Everyday Life   36
5   Virtual Realities and Augmented Experiences   43

III   Environmental Challenges and Solutions

6   Climate Crisis and Geoengineering   51
7   Sustainable Living and Green Innovations   67
8   Preserving Biodiversity in a Changing World   85

IV   Advancements in Space Exploration

9   Colonizing New Worlds   91
10   Interplanetary Travel and Beyond   95

V   Future of Medicine and Healthcare

11 Medical Breakthroughs and Longevity   101
12 Revolutionizing Healthcare Delivery   114

VI Societal Paradigm Shifts

13 Global Governance and Diplomacy   133
14 Cultural Blending and Identity in a Connected World   149

VII Ethical Dilemmas and Moral Choices

15 Artificial Intelligence and Ethics   165
16 Bioethics in an Era of Genetic Engineering   178

VIII Transforming Industries

17 Automation and the Future of Work   193
18 Energy Revolution and Clean Technologies   201

IX Human Enhancement and Transhumanism

19 Augmenting the Human Body and Mind   217
20 Ethical Boundaries of Transhumanism   224

X Reflections on the Journey

21 Epilogue: Looking Back, Looking Forward   231

Foreword

Welcome to "2100: Exploring the World of 2100." This book is a captivating journey into the realms of imagination, where we venture beyond the boundaries of our present reality and delve into the possibilities that await us in the year 2100.

As we stand on the threshold of a new era, it is essential to envision the future with a sense of wonder and curiosity. The world of 2100 holds tremendous potential for transformation, innovation, and progress. It is a world shaped by the convergence of science, technology, and human ingenuity.

In these pages, you will embark on an immersive exploration of the advancements that will shape our future. From artificial intelligence and virtual realities to renewable energy and interstellar travel, we will unravel the tapestry of possibilities that lie ahead.

But this book is more than a collection of speculative ideas. It is a call to reflect on the profound impact of our choices and actions. The challenges we face today, from climate change to social inequalities, demand our attention and inspire us to envision a future that is sustainable, equitable, and harmonious.

"2100: Exploring the World of 2100" invites us to consider the ethical dilemmas, the moral responsibilities, and the potential pitfalls that accompany progress. It prompts us to think critically about how we can navigate the ever-changing landscape of technology, science, and societal advancements in a way that serves the collective good.

Throughout these pages, you will encounter visions of hope, innovation, and resilience. You will witness the potential for human potential to overcome adversity and shape a better future for all. As you delve into the chapters that follow, let your imagination soar, your curiosity guide you, and your sense of wonder ignite.

Together, let us embark on this extraordinary journey into the world of 2100, where the possibilities are boundless, and our collective aspirations can shape the course of history.

Preface

In the vast expanse of time, the year 2100 stands as a symbol of the future—an era that holds both promise and uncertainty. It is a time that sparks our imagination and fuels our desire to explore the uncharted territories of what lies ahead.

In "2100: Exploring the World of 2100," we embark on a remarkable journey through the realms of speculation and foresight. This book is a testament to human curiosity and our innate drive to understand and shape the world around us. It is a collection of visions, ideas, and possibilities that invite us to contemplate the future with open minds and boundless enthusiasm.

Through meticulous research, informed speculation, and creative story-telling, this book paints a vivid picture of what the world of 2100 might look like. It is a tapestry woven with threads of technological advancements, environmental challenges, societal transformations, and ethical dilemmas. Within these pages, we explore the frontiers of science, contemplate the impact of our actions, and ponder the essence of what it means to be human in an ever-evolving world.

While we must acknowledge the speculative nature of these narratives, we must also recognize the importance of envisioning the future. By peering into the realm of possibilities, we gain insights into the choices and decisions that shape our present. We become conscious architects of our own destiny, mindful of the ripple effects our actions can have on generations to come.

This book is an invitation—a call to engage in thoughtful conversations, to challenge assumptions, and to imagine alternative futures. It is an exploration of the intersections between technology, ethics, environment, and society, as we navigate the complex landscape of the 22nd century.

As you embark on this immersive journey, I encourage you to embrace the spirit of inquiry and reflection. Let your mind wander and your imagination take flight. Engage in conversations with fellow readers, share your insights, and together, let us shape a future that embraces our collective aspirations for a better world.

I extend my heartfelt gratitude to the contributors, researchers, and visionaries who have helped bring this book to life. Their dedication, expertise, and passion for the future have enriched these pages with invaluable insights.

May "2100: Exploring the World of 2100" inspire us all to embrace our roles as stewards of the future and empower us to create a world that reflects our deepest values, aspirations, and dreams.

Acknowledgement

Writing a book of this nature requires the collaborative effort and support of many individuals. I would like to express my heartfelt appreciation to everyone who has contributed to the making of "2100: Exploring the World of 2100."

I am grateful to the researchers and experts in various fields who have shared their insights and knowledge. Your expertise has enriched the content of this book and has helped shape a more comprehensive understanding of the future.

I would also like to extend my gratitude to the editors and proofreaders who have diligently reviewed and refined the manuscript. Your attention to detail and commitment to maintaining the integrity of the content is deeply appreciated.

To my friends and family, thank you for your unwavering support and encouragement. Your belief in me and this project has been a constant source of motivation.

Lastly, I want to express my profound gratitude to the readers of this book. Your curiosity and engagement with the topics discussed herein inspire me to continue exploring the frontiers of the future. It is my sincere hope that this book sparks meaningful conversations and stimulates your imagination about the possibilities that lie ahead.

Together, let us embark on this journey into the world of 2100 and embrace the challenges and opportunities it presents.

I

The Dawn of a New Era

1

Prologue: A Glimpse into the Future

In the opening chapter of "2100: Exploring the World of 2100," readers are transported to a world beyond their own time. This prologue sets the stage for an exhilarating journey into the unknown, offering a tantalizing glimpse into the wonders and challenges that lie ahead.

Through evocative storytelling and vivid imagery, the prologue paints a captivating picture of the year 2100. It presents a future where technological marvels have become seamlessly integrated into everyday life, where artificial intelligence is as ubiquitous as the air we breathe, and where virtual realities blur the lines between the physical and digital realms.

Readers are invited to step into this brave new world, witnessing the marvels of advanced technology that have reshaped the human experience. They encounter intelligent personal assistants that anticipate their needs, holographic displays that bring information to life, and interconnected devices that seamlessly communicate with one another.

However, amidst the awe-inspiring advancements, the prologue also hints at the complexities and challenges that arise in this future era. It offers glimpses of environmental landscapes transformed by climate change, prompting readers to contemplate the urgent need for sustainable practices and innovative solutions.

As readers navigate this tantalizing glimpse into the future, they are encouraged to reflect on the implications of such advancements on humanity.

Questions arise about the impact of technology on personal relationships, privacy, and the very essence of what it means to be human.

The prologue leaves readers with a sense of anticipation, yearning to delve deeper into the chapters that lie ahead. It serves as a gateway, piquing curiosity and setting the stage for the thought-provoking exploration of the world of 2100 that awaits in the subsequent chapters.

With its captivating storytelling and a blend of awe-inspiring possibilities and thought-provoking challenges, Chapter 1: Prologue: A Glimpse into the Future serves as an enticing introduction to the remarkable journey that lies ahead in "2100: Exploring the World of 2100." It leaves readers hungry for more, eager to dive into the subsequent chapters and unlock the secrets and revelations of the future.

The future has always been a subject of fascination and curiosity for humankind. We yearn to peek beyond the veil of time, to catch a glimpse of what lies ahead. While the future remains uncertain, advancements in various fields give us hints about the possibilities that await us.We embark on a journey into the unknown, exploring the potential marvels and challenges that may shape the world of tomorrow.

Technological Advancements: One of the most exciting aspects of the future is undoubtedly the rapid advancement of technology. From artificial intelligence to quantum computing, we are witnessing breakthroughs that were once confined to the realms of science fiction. Imagine a future where self-driving cars seamlessly navigate bustling city streets, where virtual and augmented realities immerse us in entirely new worlds, and where medical innovations enable personalized treatments tailored to our genetic makeup.

Sustainable Living and Environmental Stewardship: As we face the pressing challenges of climate change, the future beckons us to embrace sustainable practices and become better stewards of the environment. Clean energy solutions, such as solar and wind power, are set to replace fossil fuels, leading to a significant reduction in carbon emissions. Innovations in waste management and recycling offer hope for a cleaner and greener future. Imagine cities adorned with vertical gardens, where sustainable architecture harmonizes with nature, and renewable energy sources power the bustling urban centers.

Exploring the Cosmos: The allure of space has captivated human imagination for centuries. In the future, space exploration is set to reach new heights. Humans may establish colonies on the moon and Mars, paving the way for interplanetary civilization. Exciting ventures like asteroid mining hold the potential to unlock vast resources and push the boundaries of scientific discovery. Perhaps one day, we will gaze upon distant exoplanets and ponder the existence of extraterrestrial life.

Human Augmentation and Medical Breakthroughs: Advancements in medical technology will revolutionize healthcare in the future. Imagine a world where genetic editing and regenerative medicine can eradicate hereditary diseases and extend human lifespan. Bionic limbs and neural implants may enhance human capabilities, enabling individuals to overcome physical limitations and explore new frontiers of human potential. However, ethical considerations will accompany these advancements, prompting us to tread carefully as we navigate the boundaries of human augmentation.

Cultural Blending and Global Connectivity: The future promises a world more interconnected than ever before. Advancements in communication technology will bring people from different cultures and backgrounds closer together. Cultural blending will give rise to a rich tapestry of global traditions, fostering a sense of shared humanity and understanding. However, we must also address the challenges that come with increased connectivity, such as privacy concerns and the need for digital security.

2

Shaping the Path: Socioeconomic Transformations

Socioeconomic transformations have long played a pivotal role in shaping the course of human history. As we look to the future, these transformations take on even greater significance, presenting us with both challenges and opportunities. In this article, we delve into the dynamic realm of socioeconomic changes and explore how they can pave the way for a prosperous and inclusive future.

The Digital Revolution: The rapid advancement of technology, particularly the digital revolution, has transformed the way we live, work, and interact. The rise of automation and artificial intelligence has the potential to reshape industries, creating new job opportunities while displacing others. As we navigate this transformative landscape, it becomes crucial to ensure that technological advancements are harnessed in a way that benefits society as a whole. This includes reimagining education systems to foster digital literacy and providing support for displaced workers through upskilling and retraining programs.

The digital revolution has been an ongoing phenomenon that has reshaped the world as we know it. As we peer into the future, the year 2100 holds the promise of even more profound advancements in technology, marking a new era in human history. In this article, we explore the potential impact of the digital revolution in 2100 and the transformative changes it may bring to every aspect of our lives.

Ubiquitous Connectivity: By 2100, connectivity will likely be a fundamental aspect of human existence. The proliferation of the Internet of Things (IoT) will lead to a seamlessly interconnected world, where devices, objects, and even living spaces are connected, forming an intricate web of data exchange. Individuals will experience a level of connectivity that transcends boundaries, enabling instant communication, access to information, and the integration of technology into every aspect of daily life.

Artificial Intelligence and Automation: Artificial Intelligence (AI) will have advanced to unprecedented levels by 2100. Intelligent machines, powered by neural networks and advanced algorithms, will permeate various industries, revolutionizing the workforce. Automation will have transformed many jobs, with AI-driven systems handling routine tasks, freeing humans to engage in more creative and complex endeavors. This shift will require new skills and a reimagining of education to ensure individuals can thrive in this AI-driven world.

Virtual and Augmented Realities: Virtual and augmented realities will have evolved into immersive and indistinguishable experiences from the physical world. By 2100, these technologies will have transformed entertainment, education, and even how we interact with our surroundings. Virtual class-rooms will offer immersive learning environments, allowing students to explore historical events or scientific concepts firsthand. Augmented reality overlays will enhance our perception of the physical world, blending digital information seamlessly into our everyday lives.

Healthcare and Personalized Medicine: The digital revolution will bring unprecedented advancements to the healthcare industry. By 2100, medical diagnoses and treatments will be heavily influenced by AI and big data analytics. Wearable devices and sensors will continuously monitor our health, providing real-time insights and early detection of potential issues. Personalized medicine will be the norm, with treatments tailored to an individual's unique genetic makeup, leading to more effective and precise healthcare interventions.

Ethical and Privacy Considerations: With great technological advance-ments come ethical and privacy concerns. The digital revolution in 2100 will demand a robust framework to navigate these complex issues. The responsible use of AI, the protection of personal data, and the safeguarding of privacy will require constant vigilance and regulatory oversight. Striking the right balance between innovation and safeguarding individual rights will be crucial for a sustainable and ethical digital future.

The digital revolution in 2100 holds the promise of transforming every facet of human experience. From ubiquitous connectivity and AI-driven automation to virtual and augmented realities, the world will be intercon-nected in ways we can only begin to imagine. As we venture into this future, it is vital to approach these advancements with a focus on ethical considerations, privacy protection, and the equitable distribution of benefits. By harnessing the power of technology responsibly, we can shape a digital future that enhances the human experience, fosters inclusivity, and unlocks unimaginable possibilities for generations to come.

Redefining Work: The nature of work is evolving in the face of automation, AI, and the gig economy. Traditional employment structures are giving way to freelance and remote work opportunities, providing individuals with greater flexibility and autonomy. However, this shift also raises questions about job security, fair wages, and social safety nets. To shape a future where work is equitable and fulfilling, we must strive for inclusive labor policies, promote entrepreneurship, and explore innovative models such as universal basic income to ensure economic stability for all.

The world of work is on the cusp of a monumental transformation as we venture into the year 2100. Technological advancements, shifting societal norms, and evolving economic landscapes are poised to redefine the very nature of work itself. In this article, we delve into the potential changes and opportunities that lie ahead, as we reimagine work in the future.

The Rise of Automation and AI: By 2100, automation and artificial intelligence (AI) will have reached unprecedented levels of sophistication. Routine and repetitive tasks will be largely automated, allowing humans to focus on more creative, strategic, and complex endeavors. Jobs that require uniquely human skills such as empathy, critical thinking, and innovation will become highly sought after, emphasizing the importance of lifelong learning and adaptability.

Flexibility and Remote Work: Advancements in communication technology and the growing emphasis on work-life balance will reshape the traditional concept of the workplace. By 2100, remote work will be the norm rather than the exception, with individuals enjoying the freedom to work from anywhere in the world. Virtual collaboration tools and immersive technologies will bridge distances, enabling teams to work seamlessly across borders and time zones, fostering a global community of professionals.

Embracing Entrepreneurship and the Gig Economy: The gig economy will continue to thrive in 2100, offering individuals greater flexibility and independence in their work. With a rise in freelance platforms, individuals will have the opportunity to showcase their skills, work on diverse projects, and create their own career paths. Entrepreneurship will be encouraged, with support systems and resources available to nurture innovation and venture creation.

Human-Machine Collaboration: The future of work will see an increased emphasis on human-machine collaboration. As AI systems and robots become integral parts of the workforce, humans will collaborate with these technologies to augment their abilities and enhance productivity. Humans will bring their unique strengths such as creativity, emotional intelligence, and adaptability, while machines will provide computational power, data analysis, and automation, leading to synergistic and efficient work environments.

Lifelong Learning and Skill Development: The pace of technological advancement will necessitate continuous learning and upskilling throughout one's career. In 2100, individuals will engage in lifelong learning programs, leveraging emerging technologies such as virtual reality, augmented reality, and AI-powered learning platforms. These platforms will offer personalized and immersive learning experiences, ensuring that individuals remain adaptable and equipped with the necessary skills to thrive in a rapidly evolving work landscape.

Socioeconomic Safety Nets: The transition to a new work paradigm will require robust socioeconomic safety nets to ensure the well-being of all individuals. Universal basic income, accessible healthcare, and comprehensive social support systems will be key pillars of a future-oriented society, enabling individuals to pursue meaningful work and embrace entrepreneurial endeavors without fear of financial insecurity.

As we look ahead to the year 2100, the redefinition of work holds great promise for human empowerment, creativity, and fulfillment. Embracing automation, remote work, entrepreneurship, and continuous learning will unlock new possibilities and create a work environment that celebrates human potential. By embracing these changes and building inclusive support systems, we can shape a future where work is not just a means of livelihood but a source of personal growth, purpose, and collective progress.

Building Sustainable Economies: The urgent need to address climate change and environmental degradation has placed sustainability at the forefront of socioeconomic transformation. The transition to renewable energy sources, green technologies, and circular economies is essential for the long-term well-being of our planet. This transformation presents tremendous economic potential, with the creation of green jobs and the growth of sustainable industries. By embracing sustainable practices and investing in renewable infrastructure, we can forge a path towards a more resilient and environmentally conscious future.

The urgent need to address environmental challenges has become paramount as we enter the year 2100. To secure a sustainable and prosperous future, the building of sustainable economies is of utmost importance. In this article, we explore the potential strategies and transformative changes that can shape sustainable economies in the coming century.

Transition to Renewable Energy: By 2100, renewable energy sources will have taken center stage in the global energy landscape. Fossil fuels will be largely phased out, replaced by clean and renewable alternatives such as solar, wind, geothermal, and tidal power. Sustainable energy infrastructure will be widespread, supporting the transition to a low-carbon economy and mitigating the impacts of climate change. Investments in research and development will have led to breakthroughs in energy storage, making renewable energy sources even more reliable and efficient.

Circular Economy and Resource Efficiency: The concept of a circular economy, where resources are kept in use for as long as possible through recycling, repurposing, and responsible consumption, will be firmly established in 2100. Waste management systems will have evolved to minimize landfill waste, with emphasis placed on waste reduction, resource recovery, and the design of products for recyclability. Resource efficiency will be optimized across industries, reducing the strain on natural resources and minimizing environmental degradation.

Sustainable Agriculture and Food Systems: Agriculture will undergo a significant transformation in 2100, with sustainable practices at its core. Organic farming, agroecology, and vertical farming techniques will ensure food production is environmentally friendly, conserving water, reducing chemical inputs, and minimizing carbon emissions. Technology will play a crucial role in optimizing crop yields, monitoring soil health, and ensuring efficient resource utilization. Local and community-based food systems will thrive, promoting food security, biodiversity, and resilient agricultural ecosystems.

Green Technology and Innovation: The development and adoption of green technologies will be at the forefront of sustainable economies in 2100. Investments in research and innovation will drive the advancement of clean technologies in various sectors, including transportation, manufacturing, construction, and waste management. Energy-efficient infrastructure, smart cities, and sustainable transportation systems will be the norm, reducing emissions and enhancing quality of life. Collaboration between public and private sectors will foster an ecosystem of green innovation, leading to economic growth and job creation.

Responsible Consumption and Ethical Practices: In 2100, a shift in societal values will promote responsible consumption and ethical practices. Conscious consumerism, supported by transparent supply chains and labeling, will guide purchasing decisions. Businesses will adopt sustainable production models, incorporating social and environmental considerations into their operations. Social enterprises and impact investing will flourish, aligning profit with purpose and social responsibility. The principles of the circular economy, fair trade, and social justice will underpin economic transactions, fostering a more equitable and inclusive society.

International Cooperation and Policy Frameworks: The journey towards sustainable economies in 2100 will require global collaboration and effective policy frameworks. International agreements will guide nations towards common goals, addressing climate change, biodiversity loss, and resource management. Carbon pricing mechanisms, sustainable finance initiatives, and regulatory frameworks will incentivize businesses and individuals to adopt sustainable practices. Knowledge sharing, technology transfer, and capacity building will foster a collaborative approach to sustainability, ensuring no nation is left behind.

The building of sustainable economies in 2100 presents a tremendous opportunity to create a harmonious relationship between human development and environmental stewardship. Through the transition to renewable energy, circular economies, sustainable agriculture, green technology, responsible consumption, and international cooperation, we can pave the path to a flourishing future. By integrating sustainability into all aspects of economic activities, we can achieve a balance where prosperity and environmental preservation go hand in hand, ensuring a sustainable legacy for future generations.

Addressing Inequality: Socioeconomic transformation must be accompanied by efforts to address inequality and promote social justice. As we shape the future, it is vital to ensure that economic prosperity is shared more equitably. This involves reducing wealth disparities, providing access to quality education and healthcare for all, and promoting inclusive policies that empower marginalized communities. By fostering a society where everyone has equal opportunities to thrive, we can unlock the full potential of our collective human potential.

As we enter the year 2100, the persistent issue of inequality continues to challenge societies worldwide. To create a truly prosperous and just future, addressing inequality in all its forms must be a top priority. In this article, we explore the potential strategies and transformative changes that can help build a more equitable society by 2100.

1. Education and Skills Development: Universal access to quality education will be the cornerstone of addressing inequality in 2100. Comprehensive education reforms will prioritize early childhood education, bridge the digital divide, and provide lifelong learning opportunities for all. Emphasis will be placed on cultivating critical thinking, creativity, and digital literacy to equip individuals with the skills necessary to adapt to an ever-changing world.

2. Economic Empowerment and Job Opportunities: In 2100, efforts to reduce inequality will focus on creating inclusive economic systems. Governments and businesses will promote entrepreneurship, especially among marginalized communities, providing mentorship, funding, and access to resources. Job creation programs, fair wage policies, and workplace diversity initiatives will ensure equal opportunities for all, regardless of gender, race, or socioeconomic background.

3. Social Safety Nets and Universal Basic Income: Robust social safety nets will be in place to provide a safety net for vulnerable populations and reduce inequality gaps. Universal basic income (UBI) may become a reality, ensuring that every individual has a basic level of financial security and access to essential resources. This will help address

poverty, enhance social mobility, and promote equal opportunities for all members of society.

4. Gender Equality and Women's Empowerment: In 2100, gender equality will be a fundamental principle guiding societal norms and policies. Efforts will focus on eliminating gender-based discrimination, ensuring equal pay for equal work, and promoting women's representation in leadership positions. Access to reproductive healthcare, childcare support, and parental leave policies will enable women to balance family and career responsibilities on an equal footing.

5. Environmental Justice and Climate Action: Addressing environmental inequalities will be paramount in 2100, as climate change disproportionately affects marginalized communities. Environmental justice policies will ensure equitable access to clean air, water, and healthy environments. Climate action plans will prioritize vulnerable regions, implementing sustainable development practices and renewable energy solutions that create green jobs and promote community resilience.

6. Healthcare and Universal Access: In 2100, healthcare systems will strive for universal access to quality healthcare services. Efforts will focus on reducing healthcare disparities, ensuring affordable and comprehensive healthcare for all individuals. Investment in preventive care, mental health support, and healthcare infrastructure in underserved areas will contribute to a more equitable and healthier society.

7. Rethinking Governance and Decision-making: To address inequality effectively, governance structures will become more inclusive and participatory. Decision-making processes will incorporate diverse voices and perspectives, including those from marginalized communities. Transparent and accountable governance practices will foster trust and enable collective problem-solving, ensuring that policies and reforms are equitable and responsive to the needs of all.

Addressing inequality in 2100 requires a comprehensive and transformative approach that tackles economic, social, gender, environmental, and governance-related disparities. By investing in education, promoting economic empowerment, implementing social safety nets, advancing gender equality, pursuing climate action, ensuring healthcare access, and fostering inclusive governance, we can create a society that values and uplifts every individual. Building an equitable future requires collective effort, empathy, and the determination to dismantle systemic barriers, fostering a world where opportunities and prosperity are accessible to all, irrespective of their background or circumstances.

Embracing Diversity and Collaboration: In an increasingly interconnected world, diversity and collaboration become catalysts for progress. Embracing diverse perspectives, cultures, and talents fosters innovation and creativity. By nurturing inclusive societies and promoting global cooperation, we can tackle complex challenges together, leveraging the strengths of different nations and cultures. This interconnectedness allows us to build resilient economies, bridge cultural divides, and find collective solutions to global problems.

As we venture into the year 2100, the value of diversity and collaboration in shaping a harmonious and progressive society has never been more apparent. Embracing diversity goes beyond mere tolerance; it entails recognizing the inherent worth of every individual and leveraging their unique perspectives and talents. In this article, we explore the significance of diversity and collaboration in 2100 and how they can propel us towards a brighter future.

1. Cultivating Inclusive Mindsets: In 2100, fostering inclusive mindsets will be a core aspect of societal transformation. Education systems will emphasize empathy, cultural understanding, and respect for diversity from an early age. Stereotypes and prejudices will be actively challenged through inclusive curricula and educational resources that promote cross-cultural awareness. By cultivating inclusive mindsets, society will celebrate differences and recognize the value of diverse perspectives.

2. Empowering Marginalized Communities: In 2100, efforts to embrace diversity will prioritize empowering marginalized communities. Social and economic systems will work towards dismantling systemic barriers and ensuring equal opportunities for all. Affirmative action policies, targeted support programs, and inclusive hiring practices will enable individuals from underrepresented backgrounds to thrive. By addressing historical inequities, society will become more equitable and provide avenues for all individuals to contribute to their fullest potential.

3. Building Cross-Cultural Collaboration: Globalization will continue to bridge borders, bringing diverse cultures and perspectives closer together. In 2100, collaboration across cultures will be the norm rather than the exception. International cooperation, cultural exchange programs, and collaborative initiatives will foster cross-cultural understanding and create platforms for shared learning and innovation. By embracing diverse perspectives, societies will enrich their collective knowledge and creativity.

4. Promoting Gender Equality and LGBTQ+ Rights: In 2100, gender equality and LGBTQ+ rights will be integral to a diverse and inclusive society. Efforts to promote gender equality will encompass equal representation in leadership positions, pay equity, and comprehensive healthcare services. LGBTQ+ rights will be protected, and discrimination based on sexual orientation or gender identity will be eradicated. By embracing gender and sexual diversity, society will create environments where individuals can express their authentic selves without fear of discrimination or marginalization.

5. Encouraging Interdisciplinary Collaboration: In 2100, complex challenges will require interdisciplinary approaches. Collaboration across diverse fields such as science, technology, arts, and humanities will drive innovation and problem-solving. Encouraging collaboration between scientists, artists, policymakers, and community leaders will lead to holistic solutions that address societal needs. By breaking down silos and fostering interdisciplinary collaboration, society will unlock new possibilities and create synergies that drive progress.

6. Leveraging Technology for Inclusion: Technological advancements in 2100 will play a pivotal role in fostering diversity and inclusion. Accessible and inclusive technologies will ensure that individuals with disabilities can fully participate in society. AI-powered translation tools and language-learning platforms will facilitate communication across linguistic barriers, enabling diverse voices to be heard. The digital realm will be a space where individuals can express their identities and share their experiences freely.

7. Nurturing Intercultural Dialogue: Intercultural dialogue will be a fundamental aspect of embracing diversity in 2100. Platforms for open and respectful conversations will foster understanding, empathy, and cooperation. Cultural festivals, community events, and digital forums will provide spaces for individuals to share their heritage, traditions, and stories. By nurturing intercultural dialogue, society will strengthen social cohesion and build bridges between diverse communities.

Socioeconomic transformations in the future hold immense potential to shape a thriving and inclusive world. By harnessing the power of technology, promoting sustainability, addressing inequality, and fostering collaboration, we can navigate the path ahead with resilience and optimism. It is our responsibility to proactively guide these transformations, ensuring that they serve the greater good and uplift the lives of individuals and communities worldwide. Let us embrace the opportunities that lie before us and work together to shape a future that is equitable, sustainable, and prosperous for all.

II

Technological Frontiers

3

Innovations that Redefine Humanity

Chapter 3: Innovations that Redefine Humanity

Introduction:

In the year 2100, humanity stands at the cusp of transformative technologi-cal advancements that redefine our capabilities and reshape the very fabric of our existence. Innovations across various fields have not only revolutionized industries but have also had a profound impact on the human experience. In this chapter, we explore some of the remarkable innovations that have redefined humanity in the 22nd century, revolutionizing the way we live, work, and interact with the world around us.

1.Artificial Intelligence and Cognitive Computing:

Artificial Intelligence (AI) has emerged as a dominant force, transforming nearly every aspect of human life. By 2100, AI systems have become highly sophisticated, capable of complex tasks, and advanced cognitive abilities. Cognitive computing, which combines AI with neuroscience, has enabled machines to understand human emotions, engage in natural language processing, and develop advanced problem-solving capabilities. AI-powered assistants have become an integral part of daily life, providing personalized recommendations, assisting in decision-making, and enhancing productivity across industries.

2.Augmented and Virtual Reality:

Augmented Reality (AR) and Virtual Reality (VR) technologies have transcended their initial applications, becoming integral parts of various domains in 2100. AR has transformed industries such as healthcare, engineering, and education by overlaying digital information onto the physical world, enhancing real-time decision-making and learning experiences. VR has revolutionized entertainment, communication, and training by immersing individuals in virtual environments, providing realistic simulations and interactive experiences. These technologies have redefined human perception, creating new dimensions of interaction and exploration.

3.Genetic Engineering and Biotechnology:

Advancements in genetic engineering and biotechnology have unlocked unprecedented possibilities for human health and well-being. In 2100, breakthroughs in gene editing technologies have enabled precise modifications to the human genome, offering potential treatments and cures for genetic disorders. The field of regenerative medicine has flourished, with the ability to grow replacement organs and tissues, revolutionizing transplantation and improving longevity. Biotechnology innovations have also led to the development of personalized medicines, tailored to an individual's genetic profile, optimizing treatment outcomes and minimizing side effects.

Biotechnology has undergone remarkable advancements in the year 2100, transforming the fields of healthcare, agriculture, environmental conservation, and beyond. The fusion of biology, technology, and data has led to breakthrough discoveries and innovations that have revolutionized the way we understand and manipulate living organisms. In this chapter, we explore the profound impact of biotechnology in various aspects of society, including medical treatments, genetic engineering, sustainable agriculture, and environmental preservation.

· **Medical Breakthroughs:**

In 2100, biotechnology has ushered in a new era of personalized medicine and advanced treatments. Precision medicine techniques leverage genomic information to tailor therapies to an individual's unique genetic makeup, improving treatment outcomes and reducing side effects. Gene editing technologies, such as CRISPR, have enabled precise modifications of DNA, offering potential cures for genetic diseases and the ability to eradicate certain inherited conditions. Bioengineered organs and tissues have become more accessible, addressing the global shortage of organ donors and revolutionizing transplantation procedures.

· **Genetic Engineering:**

The ability to manipulate and engineer genes has revolutionized various industries in 2100. In agriculture, genetically modified crops have increased crop yields, improved nutritional content, and enhanced resistance to pests and diseases. Gene editing techniques have been used to develop disease-resistant livestock and enhance their productivity. In the realm of synthetic biology, organisms with custom-designed genetic circuits have been created to produce valuable compounds, such as biofuels, pharmaceuticals, and industrial chemicals, in a more sustainable and efficient manner.

· **Environmental Conservation:**

Biotechnology has played a pivotal role in addressing environmental challenges in 2100. Bio-remediation techniques harness the power of microorganisms to clean up polluted environments and restore ecosystems. Genetically modified organisms have been engineered to break down harmful pollutants and degrade plastics, offering potential solutions to waste management and environmental degradation. Biotechnology has also contributed to the development of sustainable alternatives to fossil fuels, such as biofuels derived from algae or waste biomass, reducing carbon emissions and mitigating climate change.

· **Human Augmentation:**

Biotechnological advancements have opened up new frontiers in human augmentation in 2100. Neurotechnology has enabled direct interfaces between the human brain and computers, leading to advancements in brain-computer interfaces (BCIs) and neuroprosthetics. BCIs allow individuals to control external devices with their thoughts, benefiting individuals with disabilities and revolutionizing human-machine interactions. Biohacking and gene therapy techniques have led to cognitive enhancements, memory augmentation, and improved physical abilities, blurring the boundaries between humans and technology.

· **Ethical Considerations:**

As biotechnology continues to advance in 2100, ethical considerations are paramount. Striking a balance between innovation and responsible use of biotechnological tools is crucial to address potential risks and ensure equitable access to the benefits. Regulation and oversight frameworks must be in place to ensure the ethical use of gene editing technologies, protect privacy and data security in personalized medicine, and prevent the misuse of biotechnology for nefarious purposes.

The biotechnology landscape in 2100 is characterized by remarkable advancements and transformative applications across various sectors. From personalized medicine to genetic engineering, sustainable agriculture to environmental conservation, and human augmentation to ethical considerations, biotechnology has reshaped our understanding of life and the possibilities it holds. As we navigate the future, responsible and ethical application of biotechnology will be essential in harnessing its potential for the betterment of humanity and the preservation of our planet.

4.Quantum Computing and Communication:

Quantum computing has ushered in a new era of computation, with the potential to solve complex problems that were previously unsolvable by classical computers. By harnessing quantum properties such as superposition and entanglement, quantum computers in 2100 have exponentially increased processing power, revolutionizing fields such as cryptography, optimization, and drug discovery. Quantum communication has also advanced, enabling secure and unbreakable transmission of information, transforming data privacy and cybersecurity.

In the year 2100, quantum computing and communication have emerged as game-changing technologies, revolutionizing the way we process information, solve complex problems, and communicate across vast distances. Quantum mechanics, with its unique principles of superposition and entanglement, has unlocked the potential for exponential computational power and secure communication protocols. In this chapter, we delve into the advancements in quantum computing and communication, exploring their transformative impact on various industries, scientific research, and the future of technology.

· Quantum Computing Power:

Quantum computing in 2100 has surpassed classical computing capabilities, enabling us to tackle complex problems that were previously intractable. Quantum computers leverage the power of quantum bits, or qubits, which can exist in multiple states simultaneously. This property of superposition allows quantum computers to perform parallel computations, exponentially increasing their processing power. In 2100, quantum algorithms have been developed to optimize logistics, simulate complex physical systems, revolutionize cryptography, and accelerate the discovery of new materials and drugs.

· Quantum Cryptography and Secure Communication:

Quantum communication has revolutionized data security and encryption in 2100. Quantum cryptography protocols exploit the principle of entanglement to ensure secure communication channels. Quantum key distribution (QKD) allows the exchange of encryption keys encoded in quantum states, making them immune to eavesdropping attempts. The use of quantum entanglement ensures that any attempt to intercept or measure the transmitted information would disturb the quantum states, alerting both sender and receiver to the presence of an intruder. Quantum communication provides an unprecedented level of security, safeguarding sensitive information in a world with increasingly sophisticated cyber threats.

· **Advancements in Quantum Simulation:**

Quantum computing has had a profound impact on scientific research and simulation in 2100. Quantum simulators, capable of emulating complex quantum systems that are challenging to study using classical methods, have accelerated advancements in materials science, chemistry, and physics. By simulating the behavior of atoms, molecules, and quantum systems, scientists have gained insights into fundamental properties and phenomena, leading to the development of new materials with extraordinary properties, improved understanding of chemical reactions, and breakthroughs in fundamental physics.

· **Quantum Machine Learning and Artificial Intelligence:**

In 2100, quantum computing has also revolutionized the field of machine learning and artificial intelligence. Quantum machine learning algorithms leverage the power of quantum computers to process and analyze vast amounts of data more efficiently, enabling the discovery of complex patterns and relationships. Quantum-inspired algorithms have been developed to tackle optimization problems, enhancing decision-making processes, and improving predictive models. Quantum neural networks have shown promising results in pattern recognition and data classification tasks, paving the way for more advanced AI systems.

- **Quantum Internet and Global Connectivity:**

The concept of a quantum internet has become a reality in 2100, enabling secure and instantaneous communication across the globe. Quantum entanglement is harnessed to create quantum networks, where information can be transmitted instantly between entangled nodes, regardless of their physical distance. Quantum internet protocols facilitate quantum teleportation and quantum teleportation-based cryptography, enabling secure and private communication on a global scale. The quantum internet has significant implications for fields such as finance, healthcare, and government, where secure communication and data integrity are critical.

Quantum computing and communication have transformed the technological landscape in 2100, offering unparalleled computational power, secure communication, and breakthroughs in scientific research. The advancements in quantum computing power, quantum cryptography, quantum simulation, quantum machine learning, and the establishment of a quantum internet have opened up new possibilities and challenges in various industries. As quantum technologies continue to evolve, their integration into our daily lives holds the promise of solving complex problems, revolutionizing industries, and propelling humanity into a future of unprecedented

- **5.Sustainable Energy Solutions:**

With the pressing need to address climate change, sustainable energy solutions have taken center stage in 2100. Renewable energy sources such as solar, wind, and tidal power have become the primary sources of energy, significantly reducing carbon emissions and dependence on fossil fuels. Advanced energy storage technologies have made renewable energy more reliable and accessible, ensuring a stable and sustainable power supply. Innovations in energy efficiency and smart grids have optimized energy consumption, leading to greener and more resilient cities.

As the world progresses towards the year 2100, it is crucial to consider sustainable energy solutions that can reduce the impact of climate change and ensure a healthier planet for future generations. With the increasing demand for energy and the depletion of non-renewable resources, it is imperative to invest in sustainable energy sources.

One of the most promising sustainable energy solutions for 2100 is solar energy. Solar energy is renewable, abundant, and can be harnessed almost everywhere. The cost of solar technology has significantly decreased in recent years, making it more accessible for individuals and businesses. It is expected that by 2100, solar panels will be even more efficient and cost-effective, making solar energy the primary source of energy for many countries.

Another sustainable energy solution for 2100 is wind energy. Wind turbines have already proven to be an efficient and cost-effective source of energy, especially in coastal areas with consistent wind patterns. The development of more advanced wind turbine technology is expected to increase the efficiency and power output of wind turbines, making it a more viable option for energy production in the future.

Hydrogen energy is another promising sustainable energy solution for 2100. Hydrogen fuel cells are already being used in some transportation vehicles, and it is expected that hydrogen energy will become more prevalent as the technology improves. Hydrogen energy is renewable, produces no emissions, and has a high energy density, making it an attractive alternative to traditional fossil fuels.

Nuclear fusion is also a sustainable energy solution that has the potential to provide a virtually limitless source of clean energy. While nuclear fusion technology is still in its early stages of development, it holds great promise for the future of sustainable energy.

In addition to developing new sustainable energy sources, it is also essential to focus on energy conservation and efficiency in 2100. Implementing energy-efficient building designs, promoting the use of public transportation, and encouraging individuals and businesses to adopt sustainable practices can all contribute to reducing the demand for energy and reducing greenhouse gas emissions.

In conclusion, sustainable energy solutions are crucial for the future of our planet, and it is imperative to invest in renewable energy sources that can reduce the impact of climate change and ensure a healthier world for future generations. With advancements in technology and increasing global awareness of the importance of sustainability, we can look forward to a bright and sustainable energy future in 2100.

6.Neurotechnology and Brain-Computer Interfaces:

Neurotechnology advancements have transformed our understanding of the human brain and opened up new frontiers in human-computer interaction. Brain-Computer Interfaces (BCIs) have enabled direct communication between the brain and external devices, allowing individuals to control computers, prosthetic limbs, and other technologies with their thoughts. Neurostimulation techniques have shown promise in treating neurological disorders, enhancing cognitive abilities, and even exploring new frontiers of human consciousness. These innovations have revolutionized healthcare, rehabilitation, and the exploration of the human mind.

Neurotechnology and Brain-Computer Interfaces in 2100

In the year 2100, neurotechnology and brain-computer interfaces (BCIs) have revolutionized the way we understand and interact with the human brain. These advancements have opened up a new frontier in healthcare, communication, and human augmentation. By directly interfacing with the brain, neurotechnology and BCIs have the potential to enhance human capabilities, treat neurological disorders, and enable seamless communication between humans and machines. In this chapter, we explore the profound impact of neurotechnology and BCIs in various aspects of society and their implications for the future.

- **Understanding the Brain:**

Neurotechnology has significantly advanced our understanding of the human brain in 2100. Sophisticated imaging techniques, such as functional magnetic resonance imaging (fMRI) and electroencephalography (EEG), provide detailed insights into brain activity and connectivity. Advanced computational models and artificial intelligence algorithms allow researchers to decode brain signals and map neural networks, unraveling the mysteries of cognition, emotions, and behavior. This deeper understanding of the brain lays the foundation for developing effective treatments for neurological disorders and enhancing human capabilities.

- **Medical Applications:**

Neurotechnology and BCIs have transformed the field of medicine in 2100. BCIs enable direct communication between the brain and external devices, offering new possibilities for individuals with disabilities. Prosthetic limbs controlled by neural signals allow amputees to regain mobility with natural limb-like movements. Neural implants and stimulation techniques offer hope for patients with spinal cord injuries, helping them restore lost functions. Deep brain stimulation, enabled by BCIs, has shown promise in managing conditions such as Parkinson's disease and depression. Neurofeedback techniques empower individuals to regulate their brain activity, promoting mental well-being.

- **Cognitive Enhancements:**

In 2100, neurotechnology plays a crucial role in augmenting human cognitive abilities. BCIs enable direct access to brain signals associated with learning, memory, and attention. Neurofeedback training programs allow individuals to enhance their cognitive performance and improve focus. Brain stimulation techniques, such as transcranial magnetic stimulation (TMS) and transcranial direct current stimulation (tDCS), can enhance learning, creativity, and problem-solving abilities. Cognitive augmentation through neurotechnology raises ethical considerations, such as ensuring equitable access and addressing potential societal implications.

- **Communication and Human-Machine Interfaces:**

BCIs have revolutionized communication interfaces, enabling direct brain-to-machine interactions. In 2100, individuals can control digital devices, virtual reality environments, and robotic systems using their thoughts. BCIs facilitate seamless communication between humans and machines, transcending traditional input methods. This technology opens doors for individuals with disabilities, allowing them to interact with the world more independently. Additionally, neurotechnology enables brain-to-brain interfaces, facilitating direct communication between individuals through the transmission of thoughts and emotions.

- **Ethical Considerations and Privacy:**

The advancements in neurotechnology and BCIs raise significant ethical considerations in 2100. Safeguarding privacy and ensuring the responsible use of brain data becomes crucial. Clear guidelines and regulations are necessary to protect individuals' autonomy, prevent misuse of neurotechnology, and address potential issues related to cognitive enhancements and brain privacy. Ethical discussions should also encompass equitable access to neurotechnology, addressing potential social disparities and ensuring that the benefits are accessible to all.

Neurotechnology and brain-computer interfaces have ushered in a new era of understanding and interacting with the human brain in 2100. The advancements in this field hold tremendous potential for medical treatments, cognitive enhancements, and human-machine interfaces. However, ethical considerations, privacy protection, and ensuring equitable access are critical aspects that must be addressed. By harnessing the power of neurotechnology responsibly, we can improve lives, advance scientific knowledge, and unlock new frontiers of human potential.

7.Space Exploration and Interplanetary Colonization:

In the year 2100, humanity's reach extends far beyond Earth, with significant advancements in space exploration and interplanetary colonization. Robust space missions have expanded our understanding of the cosmos, uncovering new celestial bodies and unraveling the mysteries of the universe. Interplanetary colonization efforts have gained traction, with humans establishing sustainable habitats on Mars and other planets, paving the way for future civilizations beyond our home planet. These developments have redefined human aspirations, pushing the boundaries of exploration and expanding our cosmic horizons.

In the year 2100, humanity's fascination with space has evolved into an era of unprecedented space exploration and interplanetary colonization. Advancements in technology, coupled with a growing understanding of the cosmos, have propelled us towards a future where humans venture beyond Earth, seeking to establish permanent settlements on other planets and moons. In this chapter, we explore the exciting developments in space exploration and the ambitious endeavor of interplanetary colonization, envisioning a future where humanity expands its presence in the vast expanse of the universe.

- **Advancements in Space Exploration:**

By 2100, space exploration has reached remarkable heights. Robotic missions have paved the way for human exploration, with advanced spacecraft and rovers exploring celestial bodies within our solar system and beyond. Improvements in propulsion systems, such as ion drives and nuclear propulsion, have enabled faster and more efficient space travel, reducing the time required for interplanetary journeys. Exploration missions have expanded our knowledge of distant planets, moons, and asteroids, uncovering clues about the origins of the universe and the potential for habitable environments.

- **Interplanetary Colonization:**

Interplanetary colonization has become a tangible goal in 2100. Mars, with its proximity to Earth and potential for sustaining life, stands as the primary target for human colonization efforts. Advanced habitation modules and sustainable life support systems have been developed, allowing humans to establish self-sustaining colonies on the Red Planet. These colonies serve as stepping stones for further exploration and resource utilization. Moon bases have also been established, serving as research outposts and fueling stations for interplanetary missions.

- **Space Mining and Resource Utilization:**

In 2100, space mining has become a vital component of interplanetary colonization. The extraction and utilization of resources from celestial bodies, such as the Moon and asteroids, provide the necessary materials for sustaining human colonies and fueling further space exploration. Advanced mining techniques, including robotic mining operations and in-situ resource utilization (ISRU), enable the extraction of valuable minerals and water ice for life support systems and propellant production.

· **Sustainable Space Habitats:**

The establishment of sustainable space habitats is crucial for long-term interplanetary colonization. In 2100, habitats on Mars and the Moon utilize advanced technologies to create self-sustaining ecosystems. Closed-loop life support systems recycle waste, produce food, and maintain optimal living conditions for colonists. Energy generation relies on renewable sources, such as solar panels and advanced energy storage systems. The habitats prioritize efficient use of resources and minimize environmental impact, creating a blueprint for sustainable living beyond Earth.

· **Challenges and Opportunities:**

Interplanetary colonization in 2100 comes with numerous challenges and opportunities. The long-duration space travel poses risks to human health, requiring advanced medical technologies to mitigate the effects of micro-gravity and radiation exposure. The psychological and social dynamics of living in isolated and extreme environments must be carefully addressed. International cooperation and collaboration are crucial for pooling resources, knowledge, and expertise, fostering a collective effort towards exploring and settling other worlds.

Space exploration and interplanetary colonization have captured the imagi-nation of humanity in 2100. The advancements in technology, coupled with a growing understanding of the cosmos, have propelled us towards a future where humans venture beyond Earth to establish permanent settlements on other celestial bodies. Through sustainable space habitats, resource utilization, and international collaboration, we pave the way for a future where humanity expands its presence in the vast expanse of the universe, pushing the boundaries of exploration and unlocking the potential for new discoveries, scientific advancements, and the colonization of other worlds.

The innovations that redefine humanity in the year 2100 represent the culmination of centuries of scientific progress, human ingenuity, and collective collaboration. Artificial Intelligence, augmented and virtual reality, genetic engineering, quantum computing, sustainable energy solutions, neurotechnology, and space exploration have revolutionized our capabilities, transforming the way we live, work, and interact with the world around us. These innovations hold immense potential to address some of humanity's most pressing challenges, empower individuals, and reshape our future. As we continue to navigate this era of unprecedented technological advancements, it is crucial to ensure that these innovations are guided by ethical considerations, inclusivity, and a commitment to creating a better and more equitable world for all. The journey of redefining humanity in the 22nd century is not merely about technological progress; it is about shaping a future where the advancements we make truly serve the well-being and advancement of humanity as a whole.

4

Artificial Intelligence in Everyday Life

Introduction to Artificial Intelligence

Artificial Intelligence (AI) refers to the development of computer systems that can perform tasks that usually require human intelligence, such as visual perception, speech recognition, decision-making, and natural language processing. It involves the creation of intelligent machines that can simulate human thought processes and mimic human actions.

AI has been a topic of interest since the early days of computer science, with pioneers like Alan Turing proposing the idea of intelligent machines in the 1950s. However, it was not until the late 20th century that AI technology started to gain significant momentum, with the development of advanced algorithms and the availability of powerful computing resources.

Today, AI is used in a wide range of applications, from voice assistants like Siri and Alexa to self-driving cars, personalized medicine, and fraud detection in banking. It has transformed industries like healthcare, finance, and transportation, and its impact is expected to grow significantly in the coming years.

Types of Artificial Intelligence

AI can be categorized into two main types: narrow or weak AI and general or strong AI.

Narrow AI refers to systems that are designed to perform specific tasks, such as facial recognition or language translation. These systems rely on pre-defined rules and algorithms, and they can only perform the tasks they were programmed for.

General AI, on the other hand, is a more advanced type of AI that can perform a wide range of tasks and learn from new experiences. This type of AI is still in the research phase, and it is not yet commercially available.

Applications of Artificial Intelligence

AI has a wide range of applications in different industries. Here are some examples:

1. Healthcare: AI is used to develop personalized treatment plans, predict disease outbreaks, and analyze medical images.
2. Finance: AI is used for fraud detection, risk management, and investment management.
3. Transportation: AI is used for self-driving cars, traffic management, and route optimization.
4. Education: AI is used for personalized learning, automated grading, and plagiarism detection.
5. Retail: AI is used for product recommendations, inventory management, and customer service.

Challenges of Artificial Intelligence

While AI has the potential to transform industries and improve our lives, it also poses several challenges. Here are some of the key challenges:

1. Ethical concerns: AI raises questions about privacy, bias, and the impact on employment.
2. Data quality: AI relies on data, and if the data is biased or incomplete, the results can be inaccurate.
3. Regulation: As AI becomes more pervasive, there is a need for regulation to ensure that it is used ethically and responsibly.
4. Cybersecurity: AI systems are vulnerable to cyberattacks, and there is a risk that they could be used for malicious purposes.

Artificial Intelligence is a rapidly growing field with the potential to transform industries and improve our lives. While there are challenges associated with AI, there is also a tremendous opportunity to use this technology to solve some of the world's biggest problems. As AI continues to evolve, it is essential to ensure that it is used ethically and responsibly to maximize its benefits.

Machine Learning and Deep Learning

Machine Learning: The Backbone of AI

Machine learning (ML) is a subset of artificial intelligence that focuses on the development of algorithms that enable computers to learn from data and make predictions or decisions. Instead of relying on explicit programming, machine learning algorithms find patterns in data and adjust their behavior accordingly. This approach has allowed ML to become the backbone of AI and has led to groundbreaking advancements in the field.

Supervised Learning, Unsupervised Learning, and Reinforcement Learning

Machine learning can be classified into three main categories: supervised learning, unsupervised learning, and reinforcement learning.

1. Supervised Learning: Supervised learning is the most common form of ML. It involves providing the algorithm with labeled data, which consists of input-output pairs. The algorithm learns to map input to output by minimizing the difference between the predicted output and the actual output. This method is commonly used for tasks such as image classification, speech recognition, and sentiment analysis.

2. Unsupervised Learning: In unsupervised learning, the algorithm is provided with unlabeled data, and the goal is to find patterns or structures within the data. This approach is often used for tasks like clustering, anomaly detection, and dimensionality reduction. Examples of unsupervised learning algorithms include k-means clustering and principal component analysis (PCA).

3. Reinforcement Learning: Reinforcement learning is a type of ML where an agent learns to make decisions by interacting with an environment. The agent receives feedback in the form of rewards or penalties and

uses this information to improve its decision-making capabilities. This approach is particularly suitable for tasks that involve sequential decision-making, such as game playing, robotics, and autonomous vehicles.

Deep Learning: A Powerful Subset of Machine Learning

Deep learning is a subset of machine learning that focuses on the use of artificial neural networks (ANNs) to model complex patterns in data. Inspired by the structure and function of the human brain, ANNs consist of interconnected layers of neurons that process and transmit information.

The key innovation of deep learning is the use of deep neural networks, which consist of many layers of neurons. These deep architectures allow the network to learn hierarchical representations of the data, enabling the model to capture increasingly abstract features as the data moves through the layers.

Deep learning has been particularly successful in tasks that involve large amounts of unstructured data, such as image and speech recognition. Some of the most popular deep learning architectures include convolutional neural networks (CNNs) for image processing, recurrent neural networks (RNNs) for sequence data, and transformers for natural language processing.

Challenges and Future Directions

Despite the impressive achievements of machine learning and deep learning, there are still several challenges that need to be addressed:

1. Explainability: Machine learning models, especially deep learning models, are often criticized for being "black boxes" that provide little insight into how they make decisions. Developing methods to improve the explainability of these models is crucial for building trust and ensuring responsible use of AI.
2. Overfitting: ML models can sometimes become too complex and fit the training data too closely, resulting in poor performance on unseen data. Researchers are exploring techniques to mitigate overfitting and improve the generalization capabilities of models.

3. Data scarcity: Many ML models require large amounts of labeled data, which can be difficult and expensive to obtain. Researchers are working on techniques like transfer learning and data augmentation to overcome this limitation.

Artificial Intelligence in Everyday Life in 2100

Artificial Intelligence (AI) has become an integral part of our everyday lives in the year 2100, revolutionizing the way we live, work, and interact with the world around us. AI systems have advanced to a level where they can understand, learn, and make decisions with human-like intelligence, significantly enhancing various aspects of our daily routines. In this chapter, we explore the pervasive presence of AI in everyday life and how it has transformed industries, communication, transportation, healthcare, and personal assistance.

- **Intelligent Personal Assistants:**

In 2100, AI-powered personal assistants have become ubiquitous, seamlessly integrating into our daily routines. These intelligent assistants understand our preferences, anticipate our needs, and proactively assist us in various tasks. They can manage our schedules, provide real-time information, and offer personalized recommendations based on our preferences and past behaviors. With natural language processing capabilities, they can engage in fluent and contextual conversations, making interactions with technology more intuitive and human-like.

- **Smart Homes and Cities:**

AI has revolutionized the concept of smart homes and cities in 2100, creating environments that are responsive, efficient, and sustainable. AI-powered systems manage and optimize energy consumption, automatically adjusting lighting, temperature, and appliances to minimize waste. Intelligent sensors and devices enhance security and safety measures, detecting potential risks and responding proactively. AI algorithms analyze data from various sources to improve traffic management, reduce congestion, and optimize transportation routes, making cities more livable and efficient.

- **Enhanced Communication and Language Translation:**

AI has transformed communication in 2100, breaking down language barriers and enabling seamless translation between different languages. Language translation systems powered by AI can accurately interpret and translate spoken or written words in real-time, facilitating global communication and fostering cultural exchange. AI algorithms analyze and understand contextual nuances, enabling more accurate and natural translations, both in verbal conversations and written communications.

- **Intelligent Healthcare Systems:**

AI has made significant advancements in the healthcare industry, transforming patient care, diagnostics, and personalized medicine. In 2100, AI-powered systems analyze vast amounts of medical data, including patient records, research papers, and clinical trials, to provide insights and assist in disease diagnosis and treatment planning. AI algorithms can identify patterns, predict disease progression, and recommend personalized treatment options based on an individual's unique genetic makeup and medical history. AI-powered robotic assistants also support healthcare professionals in surgeries, enhancing precision and reducing risks.

- **AI in Transportation and Autonomous Vehicles:**

Transportation has undergone a revolution with the integration of AI in

2100. Autonomous vehicles powered by AI algorithms navigate roads safely, providing efficient and reliable transportation. AI systems analyze real-time traffic data, optimize routes, and enhance fuel efficiency, reducing congestion and carbon emissions. Intelligent transportation networks communicate with each other, coordinating traffic flow and anticipating potential obstacles, leading to smoother and safer journeys.

· **AI in Entertainment and Media:**

AI has transformed the entertainment and media industries in 2100, offering personalized and immersive experiences. AI algorithms analyze user preferences, behavior, and past interactions to recommend movies, music, books, and other forms of entertainment tailored to individual tastes. Virtual reality and augmented reality experiences are enhanced by AI, creating lifelike simulations and interactive storytelling. AI-powered algorithms also assist in content creation, generating personalized news feeds, and curating digital content based on individual interests.

In the year 2100, Artificial Intelligence has seamlessly integrated into our everyday lives, revolutionizing how we live, work, and interact. Intelligent personal assistants, smart homes and cities, enhanced communication, intelligent healthcare systems, AI in transportation, and AI in entertainment and media have become an integral part of our routines, enhancing efficiency, convenience, and personalization. As AI continues to advance, it is crucial to ensure ethical considerations, transparency, and human oversight, maintaining a balance between technological progress and human well-being. The impact of AI in everyday life in 2100 is indicative of the tremendous potential it holds to shape our future and create a more interconnected and intelligent world.

5

Virtual Realities and Augmented Experiences

Virtual and Augmented Reality: Transforming Our Perception of the World

Virtual Reality (VR) and Augmented Reality (AR) are immersive technologies that have the power to reshape the way we interact with digital content and the world around us. VR allows users to be fully immersed in a computer-generated environment, while AR overlays digital content onto the user's view of the real world. Both technologies have experienced rapid advancements in recent years, opening up new possibilities across various industries, including gaming, education, healthcare, and entertainment.

Virtual Reality: Immersive Digital Environments

Virtual Reality (VR) technology creates fully immersive digital experiences by simulating a user's physical presence in a computer-generated environment. Users typically wear a VR headset, which tracks their head movements and displays stereoscopic images, providing a sense of depth and immersion. Additional devices, such as hand controllers and haptic feedback systems, can further enhance the VR experience by enabling users to interact with the virtual environment and receive tactile feedback.

Applications of Virtual Reality:

1. Gaming: VR gaming has emerged as a popular application of the technology, providing players with an immersive and interactive experience that traditional gaming platforms cannot match.
2. Education: VR can be used to create immersive educational experiences, allowing students to explore historical sites, scientific simulations, or even distant planets, providing a more engaging and hands-on learning experience.
3. Training and Simulation: VR is increasingly used for training and simulation purposes in various industries, such as aviation, military, and medicine, enabling trainees to practice skills and procedures in a safe and controlled environment.
4. Mental Health and Therapy: VR has shown promise in the field of mental health, with applications such as exposure therapy for anxiety disorders and post-traumatic stress disorder, as well as pain management and rehabilitation.

Augmented Reality: Blending Digital Content and the Real World

Augmented Reality (AR) technology superimposes digital content, such as images, text, or animations, onto a user's view of the real world. AR can be experienced through various devices, including smartphones, tablets, and specialized AR headsets or glasses. By seamlessly blending digital content with the physical environment, AR can enhance our perception of the world and provide valuable context-specific information.

Applications of Augmented Reality:

1. Retail and Shopping: AR can be used to provide virtual fitting rooms, allowing customers to try on clothes or preview furniture in their homes before making a purchase.
2. Navigation and Mapping: AR can enhance navigation and mapping applications by overlaying directions, points of interest, and other relevant information directly onto the user's view of the real world.
3. Industrial and Maintenance: AR can provide technicians with real-time information, such as repair instructions or diagnostic data, overlaid on

the equipment they are working on, improving efficiency and reducing errors.

4. Entertainment and Art: AR has the potential to transform entertainment and art experiences, such as live events, exhibitions, or public installations, by adding interactive and immersive digital elements.

Challenges and Future Developments

Despite the significant advancements in VR and AR technologies, there are still challenges to overcome:

1. Hardware and Performance: Developing lightweight, comfortable, and high-performance devices that can deliver realistic and seamless experiences remains a challenge.
2. Content Creation: Creating high-quality and engaging VR and AR content requires specialized skills and tools, which can be time-consuming and expensive.
3. User Interaction and Interface Design: Developing intuitive and natural user interfaces for VR and AR is crucial to ensure accessibility and widespread adoption of the technologies.

Virtual and Augmented Reality technologies have the potential to transform the way we interact with digital content and the world around us, providing immersive and contextually relevant experiences across various industries. As advancements in hardware, software, and content creation continue, VR and AR will become more accessible

In the year 2100, the realm of virtual realities and augmented experiences has reached unprecedented heights, transforming the way we perceive and interact with the world around us. Technological advancements have led to the creation of immersive digital environments and enhanced our everyday experiences through augmented reality overlays. In this chapter, we delve into the advancements in virtual reality (VR) and augmented reality

(AR) technologies, exploring their impact on various aspects of life, from entertainment and education to healthcare and communication.

- **Immersive Entertainment:**

In 2100, entertainment has transcended traditional boundaries, offering immersive experiences that transport individuals to fantastical realms. Virtual reality has become the medium of choice for gaming, allowing players to fully immerse themselves in virtual worlds, interacting with lifelike characters and environments. With advancements in haptic feedback and sensory stimulation, users can feel the impact of virtual objects and experience heightened levels of engagement and excitement. Augmented reality has also revolutionized entertainment, with AR-enhanced live performances, interactive storytelling, and personalized experiences that blend the real and digital worlds seamlessly.

- **Transforming Education:**

Education in 2100 has been transformed by virtual realities and augmented experiences, creating engaging and interactive learning environments. Virtual reality simulations provide students with realistic and immersive educational experiences, enabling them to explore historical events, visit far-off places, and engage in hands-on experiments. Augmented reality overlays enrich traditional textbooks, bringing static images to life and offering additional information and interactive elements. Students can collaborate with peers from around the world in virtual classrooms, fostering global connections and cultural understanding.

- **Enhanced Healthcare:**

Virtual realities and augmented experiences have revolutionized healthcare in 2100, enhancing diagnostics, treatments, and patient care. Surgeons can perform complex procedures using VR-guided surgical systems, improving precision and reducing risks. Patients can undergo virtual rehabilitation programs, immersing themselves in interactive simulations that aid in recovery and improve motor skills. Augmented reality overlays provide real-time patient information to healthcare professionals, facilitating accurate diagnoses and personalized treatments. Mental health therapies leverage virtual environments to create safe spaces for patients to confront and manage their fears and anxieties.

· **Collaborative Workspaces:**

Virtual realities and augmented experiences have transformed the way we collaborate and work in 2100. Virtual reality workspaces enable teams to collaborate in immersive environments regardless of their physical locations, fostering global collaboration and reducing travel costs. Augmented reality overlays facilitate real-time information sharing and collaboration, allowing professionals to overlay digital annotations and instructions onto physical objects or spaces. Remote meetings and conferences take on a new dimension, with participants feeling as if they are physically present in a shared virtual environment.

· **Cultural Preservation and Tourism:**

In 2100, virtual realities and augmented experiences have become powerful tools for cultural preservation and tourism. VR technologies allow individuals to explore historical landmarks and cultural heritage sites that may no longer exist or are inaccessible due to various factors. Augmented reality overlays provide historical context and interactive elements to physical landmarks, enriching the tourist experience and fostering cultural appreciation. Virtual museums and exhibitions offer immersive journeys through art, history, and science, providing individuals with the opportunity to engage with cultural artifacts from around the world.

· **Social Connectivity and Communication:**

Virtual realities and augmented experiences have redefined social connectivity and communication in 2100, transcending physical boundaries and enhancing interpersonal interactions. Virtual social platforms enable individuals to connect, interact, and engage in shared activities, fostering a sense of community and belonging. Augmented reality overlays integrate digital information into social interactions, enhancing communication and providing context-specific information. From virtual gatherings and shared experiences to virtual reality dating, these technologies have revolutionized the way we connect with others and form relationships.

III

Environmental Challenges and Solutions

6

Climate Crisis and Geoengineering

In the year 2100, the Earth is grappling with the severe consequences of the ongoing climate crisis. Rising global temperatures, extreme weather events, and the depletion of natural resources have pushed humanity to explore innovative solutions to mitigate the impacts of climate change. Geoengineering, the deliberate modification of the Earth's climate system, has emerged as a controversial yet potentially vital tool in combating the crisis. In this chapter, we delve into the concept of geoengineering and its role in addressing the climate crisis in 2100.

 · **Understanding the Climate Crisis:**

By 2100, the climate crisis has reached a critical stage, with widespread consequences affecting ecosystems, economies, and human lives. Rising greenhouse gas emissions, primarily from human activities, have amplified the greenhouse effect and accelerated global warming. The Earth's climate system has undergone significant changes, including sea-level rise, melting polar ice caps, and shifts in precipitation patterns. Understanding the complexities of the climate crisis is essential for implementing effective solutions.

In the year 2100, the world finds itself grappling with the dire consequences of the climate crisis. The Earth's climate system has undergone significant changes due to human-induced factors, pushing the planet to the brink of ecological and societal disruption. Understanding the complex dynamics of the climate crisis is paramount in addressing its causes, mitigating its impacts, and charting a sustainable future. In this chapter, we explore the multifaceted aspects of the climate crisis in 2100, shedding light on its underlying factors, consequences, and the urgent need for collective action.

Causes of the Climate Crisis:

By 2100, it is widely acknowledged that human activities are the primary drivers of the climate crisis. The excessive burning of fossil fuels, such as coal, oil, and natural gas, releases large amounts of carbon dioxide (CO_2) and other greenhouse gases into the atmosphere. Deforestation, industrial processes, and agricultural practices contribute to the release of additional greenhouse gases, including methane and nitrous oxide. The cumulative effect of these emissions traps heat in the Earth's atmosphere, leading to global warming.

Consequences of Global Warming:

Global warming has far-reaching consequences for ecosystems, economies, and human well-being in 2100. Rising temperatures have resulted in the melting of polar ice caps, causing a significant rise in sea levels and threatening coastal communities and low-lying regions. Extreme weather events, such as heatwaves, hurricanes, droughts, and floods, have become more frequent and intense, posing risks to agriculture, water resources, and infrastructure. Biodiversity loss and ecosystem degradation further exacerbate the crisis, disrupting ecological balance and compromising vital ecosystem services.

As the Earth continues to warm due to the accumulation of greenhouse gases in the atmosphere, the consequences of global warming become increasingly pronounced. By 2100, the impacts of climate change are expected to have far-reaching implications for ecosystems, economies, and human societies worldwide. In this article, we explore the potential consequences of global warming in 2100, shedding light on the challenges and urgencies we face in mitigating and adapting to a rapidly changing climate.

Rising Sea Levels and Coastal Flooding:

One of the most significant consequences of global warming in 2100 is the rise in sea levels. As temperatures increase, polar ice caps and glaciers melt, leading to the influx of water into the oceans. This phenomenon threatens coastal regions, low-lying islands, and heavily populated areas, resulting in increased coastal flooding, erosion, and loss of land. Communities living in these vulnerable areas face the risk of displacement, economic disruption, and loss of vital infrastructure.

Extreme Weather Events:

Global warming amplifies the frequency and intensity of extreme weather events, such as heatwaves, droughts, hurricanes, and heavy rainfall. In 2100, these events are expected to become more frequent, posing significant challenges to agriculture, water resources, and infrastructure. Heatwaves can lead to heat-related illnesses and fatalities, while droughts can cause water scarcity, crop failures, and food insecurity. Intense rainfall and storms can result in flash floods, landslides, and damage to buildings and infrastructure.

Disruption of Ecosystems and Biodiversity Loss:

The warming climate in 2100 has severe implications for ecosystems and biodiversity. Many species face challenges in adapting to changing climatic conditions, leading to shifts in their habitats and potential extinction. Coral reefs, which support a diverse array of marine life, are particularly vulnerable to rising sea temperatures and ocean acidification. Terrestrial ecosystems, such as forests and grasslands, face increased risks of wildfires, insect infestations, and changes in vegetation patterns, impacting the balance of ecosystems and the services they provide.

Impact on Agriculture and Food Security:

Agriculture, a fundamental sector for global food production, is heavily impacted by global warming. Changes in temperature, rainfall patterns, and the prevalence of pests and diseases pose significant challenges to crop yields and livestock productivity. In 2100, agricultural regions may experience reduced crop yields, decreased nutritional value of crops, and an increased risk of food shortages. This can lead to food price volatility, malnutrition, and social unrest, particularly in regions heavily reliant on agriculture for sustenance and livelihoods.

Health Risks and Disease Spread:

Global warming in 2100 has implications for human health, both directly and indirectly. Heatwaves and extreme temperatures can lead to heat-related illnesses and heatstroke. Changes in rainfall patterns and temperatures can impact the distribution of disease vectors, such as mosquitoes, leading to the spread of diseases like malaria, dengue fever, and Zika virus. Additionally, disruptions in water availability and sanitation systems can increase the risk of waterborne diseases. Vulnerable populations, including the elderly, children, and those with pre-existing health conditions, are particularly at risk.

Impacts on Human Societies:

The climate crisis in 2100 has profound social and economic implications. Displacement of populations due to sea-level rise and extreme weather events puts a strain on infrastructure and resources, leading to increased migration and potential conflicts. Agricultural productivity is jeopardized as changing rainfall patterns and heat stress impact crop yields. Health risks escalate as the spread of vector-borne diseases and heat-related illnesses intensify. The unequal distribution of these impacts exacerbates social inequalities and poses challenges for sustainable development.

In the year 2100, human societies find themselves grappling with the profound impacts of a changing climate. The consequences of global warming, driven by human activities and the accumulation of greenhouse gases, are reshaping social, economic, and cultural landscapes around the world. In this article, we explore the potential impacts on human societies in 2100, shedding light on the challenges and opportunities that lie ahead as we navigate a rapidly changing world.

Displacement and Migration:

One of the most significant impacts of global warming on human societies in 2100 is the displacement of populations. Rising sea levels, increased frequency of extreme weather events, and changing climatic conditions can render certain regions uninhabitable or inhospitable for human settlement. This can lead to mass migration, as communities are forced to relocate to safer areas. The movement of people can strain resources and infrastructure in receiving regions, giving rise to socio-economic and political challenges.

Economic Disruption:

Global warming poses significant economic challenges in 2100. The impacts of climate change, such as reduced agricultural productivity, disruptions in supply chains, and increased costs for infrastructure maintenance and adaptation, can lead to economic instability. Industries reliant on natural resources, such as agriculture, fisheries, and tourism, may suffer declines or face the need for significant adaptation. Developing countries, in particular, may face increased vulnerability due to limited resources and infrastructure to cope with climate-related challenges.

Food and Water Security:

Changes in temperature and rainfall patterns have profound implications for food and water security in 2100. The agricultural sector may experience reduced crop yields, increased susceptibility to pests and diseases, and changes in the distribution of suitable growing regions. This can result in food shortages, price volatility, and increased competition for resources. Similarly, altered precipitation patterns can impact water availability, leading to water scarcity, particularly in regions already prone to aridity. Ensuring equitable access to safe and sufficient food and water resources becomes a pressing challenge.

Health Risks and Disease Burden:

The health impacts of global warming in 2100 are significant. Increased frequency and intensity of heatwaves can lead to heat-related illnesses and fatalities. Changes in the distribution of disease vectors and the spread of infectious diseases pose additional risks. Waterborne diseases, vector-borne illnesses, and respiratory problems can become more prevalent in regions experiencing changing climate conditions. Vulnerable populations, including the elderly, children, and those with limited access to healthcare, are particularly at risk. Strengthening public health systems and implementing climate-resilient healthcare strategies become critical priorities.

Social Inequality and Justice:

The impacts of global warming in 2100 are not evenly distributed, exacerbating social inequality and injustice. Marginalized communities, including low-income populations, indigenous peoples, and marginalized ethnic groups, are often disproportionately affected by climate change due to their limited resources, vulnerabilities, and geographical locations. Climate action and adaptation measures must be inclusive and consider the needs of these vulnerable populations, ensuring equitable access to resources, information, and decision-making processes.

Feedback Loops and Tipping Points:

Scientists have identified feedback loops and tipping points that amplify the effects of the climate crisis in 2100. Positive feedback loops, such as the release of methane from thawing permafrost or the reduction of reflective ice surfaces, contribute to further warming. Tipping points, where irreversible changes occur in the climate system, such as the collapse of major ice sheets, can lead to cascading effects with severe consequences. Understanding these feedback mechanisms and tipping points is crucial for effective climate action and preventing catastrophic outcomes.

Feedback loops are self-reinforcing mechanisms in the climate system that either amplify or dampen the effects of global warming. Positive feedback loops occur when a change in one component of the climate system leads to further changes that reinforce the initial warming trend. For example, as temperatures rise, the melting of Arctic ice exposes darker surfaces, such as open water, which absorb more heat, leading to further warming. This amplifies the initial warming trend. Other positive feedback loops include the release of methane from thawing permafrost and the reduction of reflective ice surfaces.

On the other hand, negative feedback loops work to counterbalance the warming effects and stabilize the climate system. For instance, increased atmospheric carbon dioxide (CO_2) levels stimulate plant growth and photosynthesis, which can absorb some of the excess CO_2, mitigating the greenhouse effect. However, the capacity of negative feedback loops to offset the positive feedback loops is limited, especially as global warming intensifies.

Tipping points represent critical thresholds in the climate system beyond which abrupt and irreversible changes occur. Once these thresholds are crossed, the system can undergo a dramatic transformation, leading to cascading effects with severe consequences. Tipping points can involve the collapse of major ice sheets, disruption of ocean circulation patterns, or the dieback of critical ecosystems such as coral reefs or Amazon rainforest.

The impacts of reaching tipping points are far-reaching. For example, the melting of the Greenland Ice Sheet could raise global sea levels by several meters, leading to the displacement of coastal populations and the loss of valuable coastal ecosystems. The disruption of ocean circulation patterns, such as the Atlantic Meridional Overturning Circulation, could significantly alter regional climates and impact global weather patterns. These tipping points pose enormous challenges for societies and ecosystems, emphasizing the urgency of preventing their occurrence.

Addressing feedback loops and tipping points requires a comprehensive approach that combines mitigation and adaptation strategies. Mitigation efforts focus on reducing greenhouse gas emissions to prevent further warming and limit the amplification of feedback loops. This involves transitioning to renewable energy sources, enhancing energy efficiency, and adopting sustainable practices across sectors.

Adaptation strategies aim to build resilience in human and natural systems to cope with the changing climate. This includes implementing nature-based solutions, improving water management, enhancing agricultural practices, and developing climate-resilient infrastructure. Early warning systems, disaster preparedness, and community engagement are crucial elements of effective adaptation measures.

In 2100, the planet is at a critical juncture. The feedback loops and tipping points we face demand swift and decisive action to reduce greenhouse gas emissions and limit global warming. Delaying action increases the risk of surpassing critical thresholds and tipping points, making it more challenging to prevent irreversible changes.

International cooperation, ambitious climate policies, technological advancements, and societal engagement are essential in addressing feedback loops and tipping points. Collaboration between governments, businesses, communities, and individuals is crucial to drive the necessary systemic changes and ensure a sustainable future for generations to come.

The Role of Mitigation and Adaptation:

Mitigation and adaptation strategies are essential components of addressing the climate crisis in 2100. Mitigation efforts focus on reducing greenhouse gas emissions through transitioning to renewable energy sources, improving energy efficiency, and adopting sustainable practices across sectors. This requires transformative changes in energy systems, transportation, land use, and industrial processes. Adaptation involves building resilience in communities and ecosystems, implementing nature-based solutions, and enhancing adaptive capacity to cope with the impacts of climate change.

The Role of Mitigation and Adaptation in Addressing Climate Change

Introduction:

Climate change is one of the most pressing challenges of our time, with far-reaching impacts on ecosystems, economies, and societies. To effectively tackle this global issue, a comprehensive approach that combines both mitigation and adaptation strategies is crucial. In this article, we explore the roles of mitigation and adaptation in addressing climate change and building resilience in the face of its impacts.

Mitigation:

Mitigation refers to efforts aimed at reducing greenhouse gas (GHG) emissions and minimizing the causes of climate change. The primary goal of mitigation is to limit the extent of global warming by decreasing the concentration of GHGs in the atmosphere. Key mitigation strategies include:

1. Transition to Renewable Energy: Shifting from fossil fuels to renewable energy sources such as solar, wind, and hydroelectric power can significantly reduce GHG emissions associated with electricity generation and transportation.

2. Energy Efficiency: Improving energy efficiency in buildings, industries, and transportation can reduce energy consumption and, consequently,

the associated emissions.

3. Sustainable Land Use: Implementing sustainable land management practices, such as afforestation, reforestation, and avoiding deforestation, can help sequester carbon dioxide from the atmosphere and mitigate emissions.

4. Carbon Capture and Storage (CCS): CCS technologies capture CO_2 emissions from power plants and industrial processes and store them underground, preventing their release into the atmosphere.

Mitigation measures are crucial for limiting the long-term impacts of climate change. By reducing GHG emissions, we can slow down the rate of global warming, decrease the severity of extreme weather events, and mitigate the risks to ecosystems and human societies.

Adaptation:

Adaptation involves adjusting societal and ecological systems to cope with the current and projected impacts of climate change. It focuses on building resilience and enhancing the ability of communities, ecosystems, and economies to withstand and recover from climate-related disruptions. Key adaptation strategies include:

1. Climate-Resilient Infrastructure: Designing and implementing infrastructure that can withstand the impacts of climate change, such as stronger and more resilient buildings, flood management systems, and coastal defenses.

2. Water Management: Developing sustainable water management strategies to address changing precipitation patterns, water scarcity, and the increased frequency of droughts and floods.

3. Agricultural Adaptation: Implementing climate-smart agricultural practices, such as precision farming, crop diversification, and improved irrigation techniques, to enhance food security and agricultural resilience.

4. Ecosystem-Based Adaptation: Preserving and restoring natural ecosystems, such as wetlands and forests, that provide essential services and

act as natural buffers against climate impacts.

5. Risk Assessment and Early Warning Systems: Enhancing monitoring, forecasting, and early warning systems to improve preparedness and response to climate-related hazards.

Adaptation measures help communities and ecosystems adapt to the changes that are already occurring and reduce their vulnerability to future climate impacts. They promote resilience, protect livelihoods, and ensure the well-being of communities in the face of a changing climate.

The Synergy between Mitigation and Adaptation:

Mitigation and adaptation are not mutually exclusive; they are complementary approaches that reinforce each other. By reducing GHG emissions through mitigation, we can decrease the magnitude of future climate impacts, thereby reducing the need for extensive adaptation measures. Simultaneously, adaptation measures can support the effectiveness of mitigation efforts by enabling societies to cope with the residual impacts of climate change.

Furthermore, integrating mitigation and adaptation strategies can lead to co-benefits, such as improved air quality, energy security, job creation, and enhanced ecosystem services. This integrated approach promotes sustainable development while addressing climate change challenges.

Addressing climate change requires a comprehensive approach that combines mitigation and adaptation strategies. Mitigation efforts aim to reduce GHG emissions and limit the causes of climate change, while adaptation measures focus on building resilience and adapting to the impacts that are already occurring.

The synergistic relationship between mitigation and adaptation is vital for effectively addressing the challenges of climate change and creating a sustainable future. By taking decisive action in both areas, we can mitigate the severity of climate impacts, protect vulnerable communities and ecosystems, and ensure a resilient and prosperous future for generations to come.

· **Mitigation Efforts:**

Efforts to mitigate the climate crisis in 2100 focus on reducing greenhouse gas emissions through widespread adoption of renewable energy sources, energy efficiency measures, and sustainable practices. Transitioning to a carbon-neutral society is of utmost importance to stabilize the climate and limit the long-term impacts. However, despite significant progress, existing mitigation strategies may not be sufficient to counteract the effects of past emissions, necessitating the exploration of alternative approaches such as geoengineering.

Mitigation efforts play a crucial role in addressing climate change by reducing greenhouse gas (GHG) emissions and minimizing the factors contributing to global warming. These efforts are essential for mitigating the impacts of climate change and transitioning towards a more sustainable and low-carbon future. In this article, we explore various mitigation strategies and their significance in tackling climate change.

One of the most effective ways to mitigate climate change is by transitioning from fossil fuels to renewable energy sources. Renewable energy, such as solar, wind, hydroelectric, and geothermal power, offers a clean and sustainable alternative to traditional energy sources that release significant amounts of GHG emissions. By investing in renewable energy infrastructure and encouraging its widespread adoption, countries can significantly reduce their carbon footprint and decrease reliance on fossil fuels.

Improving energy efficiency across sectors is another vital mitigation strategy. By optimizing energy consumption and reducing waste, we can achieve significant GHG emissions reductions. Energy-efficient practices include upgrading building insulation, using energy-saving appliances and equipment, implementing smart grid systems, and promoting energy-conscious behavior. Energy efficiency not only helps combat climate change but also leads to cost savings and resource conservation.

Transportation is a major contributor to GHG emissions, primarily through the combustion of fossil fuels in cars, trucks, ships, and airplanes. Mitigating transportation emissions involves promoting sustainable transportation options such as electric vehicles (EVs), public transit systems, cycling, and walking. Investing in EV infrastructure, expanding public transportation networks, and incentivizing low-carbon transportation modes are key strategies in reducing transportation-related emissions.

Land use change, deforestation, and degradation of natural ecosystems contribute significantly to GHG emissions. Mitigation efforts in this area focus on sustainable land management practices, afforestation, reforestation, and preserving existing forests. Forests act as carbon sinks, absorbing CO_2 from the atmosphere, and protecting them helps mitigate climate change. Sustainable agriculture practices, such as agroforestry and organic farming, can also contribute to reducing emissions from land use.

CCS technologies capture CO_2 emissions from power plants and industrial processes and store them underground, preventing their release into the atmosphere. CCS can help mitigate emissions from sectors that are challenging to decarbonize, such as heavy industries and power generation. Additionally, carbon removal technologies, such as direct air capture and enhanced weathering, can remove CO_2 from the atmosphere and contribute to mitigation efforts.

Adopting a circular economy approach aims to minimize waste generation, promote recycling and reuse, and reduce resource extraction. By implementing efficient waste management systems, including recycling programs, composting, and waste-to-energy facilities, we can reduce emissions from landfills and the production of new materials. Circular economy practices help conserve resources, decrease emissions, and contribute to sustainable development.

Mitigating emissions from industries requires transitioning to low-carbon technologies, promoting energy-efficient manufacturing processes, and reducing the use of fossil fuels. Encouraging the development and adoption of green technologies, such as clean energy solutions, sustainable materials, and advanced manufacturing techniques, can significantly contribute to emissions reduction across industrial sectors.

Mitigation efforts are crucial for reducing GHG emissions, limiting climate change, and creating a sustainable future. Transitioning to renewable energy, improving energy efficiency, promoting sustainable transportation and land use practices, investing in CCS technologies, adopting circular economy approaches, and promoting green technologies are key strategies in mitigating climate change. By implementing these measures at the individual, community, national, and international levels, we can make significant

- **Geoengineering Concepts:**

Geoengineering encompasses a range of deliberate interventions in the Earth's climate system to counteract climate change. In 2100, two main categories of geoengineering techniques are under consideration: solar radiation management (SRM) and carbon dioxide removal (CDR). SRM aims to reflect a portion of the sun's energy back into space, reducing global temperatures. CDR techniques, on the other hand, seek to remove excess carbon dioxide from the atmosphere.

As the impacts of climate change become increasingly apparent, scientists and policymakers are exploring various geoengineering concepts as potential strategies to mitigate global warming and its associated effects. Geoengineering refers to deliberate, large-scale interventions in the Earth's systems to counteract climate change. While these concepts are still in the experimental stage and come with potential risks and ethical considerations, understanding their possibilities can help inform discussions on climate change mitigation. In this article, we delve into some prominent geoengineering concepts and their potential implications.

Solar Radiation Management aims to reduce the amount of solar radiation reaching the Earth's surface, thereby counteracting global warming. One proposed method is the injection of aerosols into the stratosphere, simulating the cooling effect of volcanic eruptions. These aerosols reflect sunlight back into space, potentially lowering global temperatures. However, SRM techniques are associated with uncertainties, such as regional climate impacts, disruption of rainfall patterns, and potential side effects on the ozone layer.

Carbon Dioxide Removal techniques aim to remove CO_2 from the atmosphere, thereby reducing its concentration and mitigating climate change. Several CDR approaches are being explored, including afforestation and reforestation programs, direct air capture, ocean fertilization, and enhanced weathering. These techniques have the potential to reduce atmospheric CO_2 levels but face challenges such as high costs, limited scalability, and potential ecological and social impacts.

BECCS combines bioenergy production with carbon capture and storage. It involves cultivating biomass, such as energy crops or algae, using them for energy generation, and capturing the CO_2 emissions produced during the process for storage underground. BECCS has the potential to generate energy while simultaneously removing CO_2 from the atmosphere. However, concerns exist regarding land use competition, sustainability of biomass production, and long-term carbon storage reliability.

Ocean Alkalinity Enhancement involves adding alkaline substances to seawater to increase its capacity to absorb CO_2 from the atmosphere. This process promotes the formation of bicarbonate ions, which react with atmospheric CO2, resulting in its uptake by the ocean. While this concept shows promise, potential consequences include altering marine ecosystems, impacting marine biodiversity, and affecting ocean chemistry.

SAI involves the injection of aerosols, such as sulfur dioxide particles, into the stratosphere to create a reflective layer that reduces solar radiation reaching the Earth's surface. This concept aims to mimic the cooling effects of volcanic eruptions. However, SAI raises concerns related to its potential side effects on weather patterns, regional climate impacts, and the need for sustained deployment to counteract rising temperatures.

Geoengineering concepts offer potential strategies to address climate change, but they come with significant uncertainties and risks. While they should not be seen as a substitute for mitigation and adaptation efforts, they can complement existing strategies in combating global warming. It is crucial to conduct thorough research, assess potential risks, and consider the ethical, social, and environmental implications before deploying large-scale geoengineering interventions. Continued scientific research, robust governance frameworks, and international collaboration are necessary to ensure the responsible exploration and potential future use of geoengineering concepts as part of a comprehensive approach to addressing climate change.

· **Solar Radiation Management:**

Solar radiation management techniques in 2100 include the deployment of reflective aerosols in the stratosphere, creation of artificial clouds, and placing mirrors in space to deflect sunlight. These interventions aim to reduce the amount of solar radiation reaching the Earth's surface, thereby cooling the planet. However, SRM techniques come with potential risks and uncertainties, including regional climate impacts, disruption of precipitation patterns, and the need for ongoing maintenance and global cooperation.

- **Carbon Dioxide Removal:**

Carbon dioxide removal techniques focus on removing excess CO_2 from the atmosphere, aiming to restore a balanced carbon cycle. In 2100, advanced CDR technologies are being explored, including large-scale afforestation and reforestation efforts, direct air capture technologies, and enhanced weathering. These approaches sequester carbon from the atmosphere and store it in vegetation, soils, or geological formations. However, CDR techniques face challenges such as land availability, energy requirements, and long-term storage considerations.

- **Ethical and Environmental Considerations:**

The implementation of geoengineering techniques in 2100 raises significant ethical and environmental concerns. Geoengineering interventions could have unintended consequences, altering regional climates and ecological systems. Governance mechanisms, transparency, and international cooperation are essential to ensure responsible and ethical deployment of geoengineering technologies. Public engagement, informed decision-making, and ongoing research are necessary to understand the potential risks and benefits associated with geoengineering interventions.

In 2100, the climate crisis has forced humanity to explore innovative solutions to combat climate change. Geoengineering, although controversial and surrounded by uncertainties, offers potential tools to address the crisis. Solar radiation management and carbon dioxide removal techniques provide avenues for mitigating the impacts of global warming and stabilizing the climate. However, careful consideration of ethical, social, and environmental implications is crucial

7

Sustainable Living and Green Innovations

In the face of escalating environmental challenges, the need for sustainable living practices and green innovations has never been more critical. The year 2100 represents a pivotal moment in our collective efforts to build a resilient future, where sustainable lifestyles and innovative technologies converge to address pressing ecological concerns. This article explores the concept of sustainable living in 2100 and the remarkable green innovations that shape our daily lives.

- **Renewable Energy Revolution:**

By 2100, the world has undergone a transformative shift towards renewable energy sources. Solar panels and wind turbines are ubiquitous, harnessing clean and abundant energy from the sun and wind. Advanced energy storage systems allow for efficient utilization of renewable power, ensuring a consistent and reliable energy supply. Communities have embraced microgrids, enabling localized energy production and distribution, reducing transmission losses, and promoting self-sufficiency.

- **Smart Cities and Green Infrastructure:**

Cities in 2100 have become smart, sustainable hubs where green infrastruc-ture reigns supreme. Buildings are designed with energy-efficient materials and equipped with smart technologies that monitor energy consumption and optimize resource utilization. Vertical gardens and rooftop farms adorn urban landscapes, providing fresh produce and improving air quality. Intelligent transportation systems prioritize public transit, shared mobility, and electric vehicles, reducing congestion and emissions.

Renewable Energy Revolution in 2100: Transforming the Global Energy Landscape

1. Solar Power Dominance:

- Highly efficient and affordable solar panels cover rooftops, buildings, and vast solar farms.
- Advanced solar technologies, such as perovskite solar cells, revolutionize energy conversion efficiency.
- Solar energy storage systems, including advanced batteries and molten salt storage, ensure uninterrupted power supply.

2.Wind Power Expansion:

- Massive wind farms dot coastlines, oceans, and open landscapes, har-nessing the power of wind.
- Offshore wind turbines reach unprecedented heights and capacities, maximizing energy generation.
- Floating wind farms in deep waters become a prominent source of renewable energy.

3.Hydropower Advancements:

- Enhanced hydroelectric power systems utilize smart turbines and inno-vative dam designs.
- Run-of-river hydroelectric plants with minimal environmental impact

gain popularity.

- Tidal and wave energy technologies make significant strides, tapping into the immense power of the ocean.

4.Geothermal Innovations:

- Advanced geothermal power plants tap into deeper, hotter sources for increased energy production.
- Geothermal heat pumps provide efficient heating and cooling solutions for buildings and residential areas.
- Geothermal energy utilization extends to industrial processes and district heating systems.

5.Biomass and Bioenergy:

- Sustainable biomass sources, such as agricultural waste and algae, fuel bioenergy power plants.
- Advanced biofuel technologies enable cleaner transportation and decarbonization of industries.
- Biomass co-firing and gasification techniques contribute to energy diversification and waste management.

6.Marine Energy Harvesting:

- Tidal and current energy converters harness the immense power of the ocean's movements.
- Ocean thermal energy conversion (OTEC) systems generate electricity from temperature differences in ocean water.
- Salinity gradient power plants utilize the disparity between freshwater and saltwater to generate clean energy.

7.Energy Storage Breakthroughs:

- Advanced battery technologies, including solid-state and flow batteries, revolutionize energy storage.
- Power-to-gas systems convert excess renewable energy into hydrogen for long-term storage and use.
- Compressed air energy storage (CAES) and gravity storage systems offer scalable and efficient energy storage solutions.

8.Grid Modernization and Microgrids:

- Smart grid systems integrate renewable energy sources, storage, and demand response technologies.
- Microgrids enable localized energy generation and distribution, increasing grid resilience.
- Blockchain and decentralized energy systems facilitate peer-to-peer energy trading and grid optimization.

9.Electrification of Transportation:

- Electric vehicles (EVs) dominate the transportation sector, supported by widespread charging infrastructure.
- High-speed electric trains and hyperloop systems revolutionize long-distance travel.
- Electric aviation technologies emerge, transforming air travel with zero-emission aircraft.

10.Energy Efficiency and Demand-Side Management:

- Smart buildings equipped with energy-efficient systems, automated controls, and intelligent sensors reduce energy consumption.
- Demand-side management programs and dynamic pricing incentivize energy conservation.
- Energy-efficient appliances, lighting, and electronics become the standard in households and businesses.

The renewable energy revolution in 2100 transforms the global energy landscape, ensuring a sustainable, clean, and resilient future for all.

· Circular Economy and Zero Waste:

The concept of a circular economy has gained significant traction, with waste reduction and resource conservation at its core. 2100 sees the proliferation of advanced recycling technologies that can efficiently process various materials, from plastics to e-waste. Products are designed with longevity and recyclability in mind, promoting a culture of repair, reuse, and recycling. Zero waste initiatives and community composting programs have become the norm, minimizing landfill waste and promoting a sustainable approach to consumption.

In the face of environmental challenges and resource scarcity, the concept of a circular economy and zero waste has gained significant attention. It presents a transformative approach to our current linear consumption patterns, aiming to minimize waste generation, maximize resource efficiency, and create a regenerative and sustainable future. This essay explores the principles and benefits of a circular economy and zero waste, highlighting its potential to drive economic growth while preserving the environment.

Principles of a Circular Economy:

At its core, a circular economy is based on three fundamental principles:

1. Designing out waste and pollution: Emphasizing the importance of product design, a circular economy focuses on creating goods that are durable, repairable, and recyclable. It encourages manufacturers to adopt eco-design principles, considering the entire lifecycle of a product and minimizing waste generation.

2. Keeping products and materials in use: In a circular economy, the aim

is to extend the lifespan of products through repair, refurbishment, and remanufacturing. Embracing the concept of sharing and collaborative consumption, businesses explore innovative business models such as product leasing, rental, and sharing platforms to maximize product utilization.

3. Regenerating natural systems: A circular economy emphasizes the importance of restoring and regenerating natural resources. It promotes the use of renewable materials, encourages recycling and waste-to-energy processes, and encourages the return of organic waste to the soil through composting and anaerobic digestion.

Benefits of a Circular Economy and Zero Waste:

1. Resource Conservation: By shifting from a linear "take-make-dispose" model to a circular approach, a significant reduction in resource consumption can be achieved. Recycling, remanufacturing, and reuse reduce the need for extracting virgin resources, preserving valuable materials and reducing environmental degradation.

2. Waste Reduction: A circular economy aims to minimize waste generation by ensuring that materials are kept within the economic system. This leads to reduced landfill usage, lower pollution levels, and a more efficient use of resources.

3. Economic Growth and Job Creation: Transitioning to a circular economy presents significant economic opportunities. By developing innovative recycling and remanufacturing industries, new jobs can be created, fostering economic growth while reducing environmental impact.

4. Energy and Carbon Footprint Reduction: A circular economy reduces the demand for energy-intensive processes associated with extracting and manufacturing virgin materials. By promoting recycling and reusing, it reduces greenhouse gas emissions, contributing to mitigating climate change.

5. Improved Product Quality and Consumer Engagement: Embracing a circular economy encourages businesses to produce high-quality, long-

lasting products that can be easily repaired and upgraded. Consumers become more engaged, seeking products with longer lifespans, higher value, and reduced environmental impact.

6. Enhanced Resilience and Sustainability: A circular economy fosters a resilient and self-sustaining system. By diversifying supply chains, promoting local production, and reducing dependence on finite resources, it creates a more robust and sustainable economic framework.

Challenges and the Way Forward:

Implementing a circular economy and zero waste practices requires overcoming several challenges. These include changing consumer behavior, establishing effective waste management systems, and promoting collaboration among various stakeholders. Governments, businesses, and individuals must work together to create enabling policies, invest in research and development, and raise awareness about the benefits of a circular economy.

A circular economy and zero waste offer a compelling vision for a sustainable future. By adopting these principles, we can move beyond the linear model of consumption and waste generation, and transition to a system that values resource efficiency, environmental preservation, and economic growth. Embracing a circular economy is not only essential for addressing the pressing environmental challenges we face but also for creating a more prosperous and resilient society for future generations.

· **Sustainable Food Systems:**

In 2100, sustainable food systems have revolutionized the way we produce and consume food. Vertical farms and hydroponics dominate urban landscapes, efficiently utilizing space and reducing the need for agricultural land.

Plant-based diets have gained popularity, contributing to lower greenhouse gas emissions and improved public health. Locally sourced and organic food options are readily available, fostering a stronger connection between consumers and producers.

As the global population continues to grow and environmental challenges intensify, ensuring food security and sustainability has become a critical priority. Sustainable food systems offer a comprehensive approach that considers the social, economic, and environmental dimensions of food production, distribution, and consumption. This essay explores the importance of sustainable food systems in nourishing people and protecting the planet, highlighting key principles and practices for a more sustainable future.

Key Principles of Sustainable Food Systems:

1. Environmental Stewardship: Sustainable food systems prioritize the protection and restoration of ecosystems. They promote sustainable farming practices that minimize chemical inputs, conserve water, protect biodiversity, and reduce greenhouse gas emissions. This includes organic farming, agroforestry, and regenerative agriculture techniques that promote soil health and carbon sequestration.

2. Efficient Resource Use: Sustainable food systems aim to optimize resource use throughout the entire food supply chain. This involves reducing food loss and waste, improving water management, adopting precision agriculture technologies, and minimizing energy consumption in production, processing, and transportation.

3. Social Equity and Justice: Sustainable food systems emphasize fair and equitable access to nutritious food for all. They promote social inclusion, support local food economies, and ensure fair wages and working conditions for farmers and food workers. They also address food disparities by promoting community gardens, farmers' markets, and initiatives to combat food deserts.

4. Resilient and Diverse Production: Sustainable food systems encourage diverse and resilient agricultural practices. They promote crop rotation, polyculture, and the use of native and climate-adapted crops. These

practices help reduce the risk of crop failure, increase biodiversity, and improve ecosystem resilience in the face of climate change and other challenges.

5. Circular Economy Approaches: Sustainable food systems strive to reduce waste and promote circularity in the food chain. This involves adopting practices such as composting, anaerobic digestion, and food recycling. Additionally, promoting sustainable packaging and reducing single-use plastics contribute to waste reduction efforts.

Benefits of Sustainable Food Systems:

1. Food Security and Nutrition: Sustainable food systems ensure long-term food security by promoting diverse, nutrient-rich diets and reducing dependency on a few staple crops. They prioritize local and regional food production, reducing vulnerability to global supply chain disruptions and enhancing food sovereignty.

2. Environmental Preservation: By minimizing the use of chemical inputs, reducing greenhouse gas emissions, and preserving ecosystems, sustainable food systems contribute to environmental conservation. They protect soil health, water quality, and biodiversity, promoting the long-term sustainability of the planet.

3. Economic Opportunities: Sustainable food systems create economic opportunities by supporting small-scale farmers, local food businesses, and rural communities. They foster job creation, promote fair trade, and contribute to resilient local economies.

4. Climate Change Mitigation and Adaptation: Sustainable food systems play a vital role in mitigating climate change. They promote practices that sequester carbon in soils, reduce deforestation, and minimize the energy required for food production. Moreover, by prioritizing diverse and resilient crops, they enhance the capacity to adapt to changing climatic conditions.

Transitioning to sustainable food systems is crucial for nourishing people and protecting the planet. By adopting environmentally-friendly practices, ensuring social equity, and promoting efficient resource use, we can create a food system that is resilient, inclusive, and sustainable. Governments, businesses, farmers, and consumers all have a role to play in supporting and promoting sustainable food systems. Together, we can build a future where everyone has access to nutritious food, ecosystems are protected, and the agricultural sector thrives in harmony with nature.

· **Eco-friendly Transportation:**

Transportation in 2100 has undergone a significant transformation, with a focus on sustainable and efficient modes of travel. Electric and hydrogen-powered vehicles have replaced fossil fuel-dependent cars, reducing emissions and noise pollution. High-speed rail networks connect cities, offering a fast and sustainable alternative to air travel for long distances. Bike-sharing programs and pedestrian-friendly infrastructure encourage active transportation, enhancing physical well-being and reducing carbon emissions.

Eco-friendly Transportation in 2100: Paving the Way for Sustainable Mobility

1. Electric Vehicles (EVs): By 2100, electric vehicles are expected to dominate the transportation sector. EVs produce zero tailpipe emissions, reducing air pollution and greenhouse gas emissions. Continued advancements in battery technology will enhance their range and charging infrastructure, making them a viable and sustainable alternative to traditional internal combustion engine vehicles.

2. Hydrogen Fuel Cell Vehicles: Hydrogen fuel cell vehicles utilize hydrogen as a clean energy source, emitting only water vapor. These vehicles

have the potential to provide long-range capabilities and quick refueling times, making them suitable for various transportation needs. In 2100, advancements in hydrogen production and storage technologies could make them a mainstream option.

3. Sustainable Aviation: The aviation industry is making significant strides towards sustainability. By 2100, we can expect a transition to low-carbon and electric aircraft, fueled by renewable energy sources. Sustainable aviation fuels derived from algae, plant matter, or waste materials will replace conventional jet fuels, reducing carbon emissions and air pollution.

4. High-Speed Rail: High-speed rail systems will become more prevalent, offering efficient and eco-friendly transportation options for long-distance travel. These systems are powered by electricity and produce significantly fewer emissions compared to air or road transport. Advanced rail technologies, such as magnetic levitation (Maglev) trains, will allow for faster and smoother journeys.

5. Smart and Shared Mobility: In 2100, smart and shared mobility solutions will transform transportation systems. Autonomous vehicles, connected networks, and intelligent transportation systems will optimize traffic flow, reduce congestion, and improve overall efficiency. Car-sharing services, ride-sharing platforms, and integrated public transport systems will minimize the number of vehicles on the road, leading to reduced energy consumption and emissions.

6. Cycling and Pedestrian Infrastructure: In the future, cities will prioritize the development of comprehensive cycling and pedestrian infrastructure. Extensive networks of bike lanes, pedestrian-friendly streets, and green spaces will encourage active transportation and reduce reliance on cars. Electric bikes and scooters will also play a significant role in providing sustainable last-mile transportation options.

7. Alternative Fuels: In addition to electric and hydrogen-powered vehicles, alternative fuels such as biofuels, compressed natural gas (CNG), and synthetic fuels derived from renewable sources will contribute to a more sustainable transportation system. These fuels have lower

carbon footprints and can be used in existing vehicles with minimal modifications.

8. Smart Traffic Management: Advanced traffic management systems will optimize traffic flow, reducing idling times and fuel consumption. Real-time data, predictive analytics, and smart algorithms will allow for adaptive traffic control, minimizing congestion and emissions.

9. Vertical Mobility: Vertical mobility solutions, including advanced aerial vehicles and drones, will revolutionize urban transportation. These vehicles can alleviate traffic congestion and provide efficient transportation for short distances, enhancing last-mile connectivity and reducing emissions in urban areas.

10. Active Transportation Promotion: Governments and urban planners will actively promote walking and cycling as viable transportation modes. This includes the development of pedestrian-friendly infrastructure, bike-sharing programs, and incentives for active commuting. Encouraging active transportation not only reduces emissions but also promotes public health and well-being.

Eco-friendly transportation in 2100 will be characterized by electric vehicles, hydrogen fuel cell vehicles, sustainable aviation, high-speed rail, shared mobility, cycling infrastructure, and smart traffic management. With a focus on renewable energy sources, efficient transport systems, and reduced emissions, the transportation sector will contribute to a more sustainable and environmentally friendly future. By embracing these eco-friendly transportation solutions, we can achieve cleaner air, reduced carbon emissions, and enhanced mobility for generations to come.

· **Nature-Inspired Innovations:**

Green innovations in 2100 draw inspiration from nature, utilizing biomimicry to design sustainable solutions. Bio-inspired materials that replicate the strength and flexibility of natural fibers are widely used in construction, reducing the carbon footprint of buildings. Innovations inspired by plant photosynthesis enable efficient solar energy conversion. Sustainable packaging solutions mimic the protective properties of natural materials, reducing waste and pollution.

The natural world has long served as a source of inspiration for human innovation. In the year 2100, we can expect a profound shift towards nature-inspired technologies and design principles, known as biomimicry. By emulating nature's time-tested strategies and solutions, we can create sustainable and efficient technologies that address complex challenges facing humanity. This essay explores the concept of nature-inspired innovations and highlights some key areas where biomimicry will play a pivotal role in shaping our future.

Biomimicry: Learning from Nature's Designs:

Biomimicry involves observing and understanding nature's patterns, structures, and processes to develop innovative solutions. By studying how organisms have evolved to thrive in their environments, we can unlock nature's secrets and apply them to human-made systems. Biomimicry encompasses a wide range of disciplines, including engineering, architecture, materials science, and medicine, and holds great potential for sustainable development.

Key Areas of Nature-Inspired Innovations:

1. Energy Harvesting and Storage: Nature-inspired approaches can revolutionize the way we generate and store energy. For example, researchers are studying photosynthesis to develop more efficient solar panels that mimic the way plants convert sunlight into energy. Biomimetic battery designs inspired by the energy storage mechanisms of living organisms could lead to breakthroughs in energy storage capacity and longevity.

2. Sustainable Materials and Manufacturing: Nature provides a wealth of inspiration for developing sustainable materials and manufacturing

processes. The strength and lightweight nature of spider silk, for instance, have inspired the creation of bio-inspired materials with similar properties. Additionally, 3D printing technologies that mimic the growth patterns of coral reefs or tree branches can enable efficient and sustainable manufacturing techniques.

3. Water and Resource Management: Nature has perfected resource management over billions of years. By studying the intricate water management systems of plants, we can design innovative solutions for water conservation, filtration, and distribution. Mimicking the way desert beetles collect water from the air, we can develop self-filling water containers that harness atmospheric moisture in arid regions.

4. Smart and Resilient Infrastructure: Nature's ecosystems offer lessons in resilience, adaptability, and efficiency. By incorporating biomimetic principles, we can design smart infrastructure systems that respond to changing conditions. For example, buildings can be inspired by termite mounds, which maintain stable internal temperatures through natural ventilation systems, reducing the need for artificial cooling and heating.

5. Healthcare and Biotechnology: Nature-inspired innovations have the potential to revolutionize healthcare and biotechnology. From studying the healing properties of plants to mimicking the structure and functionality of organs, biomimicry can lead to new approaches in drug delivery, tissue engineering, and medical diagnostics. Artificial organs and prosthetics designed with inspiration from natural structures can enhance patient outcomes and quality of life.

Benefits of Nature-Inspired Innovations:

1. Sustainability: Nature-inspired innovations promote sustainability by imitating nature's efficient use of resources and minimizing waste. These technologies have the potential to reduce our ecological footprint, conserve energy, and protect biodiversity.

2. Resilience: Biomimicry enables the development of resilient systems that can adapt to changing environmental conditions. By learning from

nature's resilience strategies, we can create infrastructure, materials, and technologies that withstand natural disasters and climate change impacts.

3. Efficiency and Performance: Nature's designs are highly efficient and optimized for their specific functions. By harnessing these design principles, we can develop technologies that are more energy-efficient, lightweight, and perform at higher levels.

4. Inspiration for Innovation: Nature-inspired innovations stimulate creativity and inspire interdisciplinary collaboration. They encourage us to view the natural world as a vast library of solutions, fostering a deeper

· **Conscious Consumerism and Ethical Business Practices:**

In 2100, consumers are more conscious of their purchasing choices, prioritizing ethical and sustainable products. Companies have adopted transparent supply chains, ensuring fair trade practices and environmentally responsible sourcing. Corporate sustainability initiatives extend beyond compliance, with businesses actively contributing to the well-being of communities and ecosystems.

Conscious Consumerism and Ethical Business Practices in 2100: Shaping a Sustainable Economy

Introduction:

In the year 2100, consumer attitudes and business practices will have undergone a transformative shift towards conscious consumerism and ethical business practices. As societies become increasingly aware of the environmental, social, and ethical impacts of their consumption choices, individuals will demand transparency, sustainability, and social responsibility from businesses. This essay explores the concept of conscious consumerism and the importance of ethical business practices in building a sustainable economy for the future.

Conscious Consumerism: Empowering Choices for a Better World

Conscious consumerism is a movement that encourages individuals to make purchasing decisions aligned with their values and the greater good. In 2100, consumers will prioritize products and services that are environmentally friendly, socially responsible, and ethically sourced. They will actively seek out businesses that demonstrate a commitment to sustainability, fair trade, human rights, and animal welfare. By supporting companies that align with their values, consumers will play a crucial role in driving positive change and shaping a sustainable economy.

Key Aspects of Conscious Consumerism:

1. Sustainability: Consumers in 2100 will prioritize sustainability, seeking products and services that minimize environmental impact throughout their lifecycle. They will demand transparency regarding sourcing, production processes, and carbon footprints. Companies will respond by adopting sustainable practices such as renewable energy use, waste reduction, and responsible supply chain management.

2. Fair Trade and Ethical Sourcing: Ethical considerations will drive consumer choices, with a focus on fair trade practices and ethical sourcing of raw materials. Consumers will demand that workers along the supply chain receive fair wages, safe working conditions, and have their rights respected. Businesses will establish robust systems to ensure transparency and accountability throughout their supply chains.

3. Social Responsibility: Conscious consumers will support businesses that prioritize social responsibility. They will seek out companies that actively engage in community development, support local economies, and contribute to social causes. Businesses will integrate social impact initiatives into their core strategies, addressing social issues such as poverty, education, and inequality.

4. Transparency and Accountability: Consumers will demand greater transparency and accountability from businesses. They will expect companies to disclose their environmental and social impact, as well as their efforts towards improvement. Companies will adopt comprehensive

reporting frameworks and third-party certifications to provide credible information to consumers.

Ethical Business Practices: Redefining Corporate Responsibility

In 2100, ethical business practices will be the norm rather than the exception. Companies will recognize that long-term success and profitability are interconnected with sustainable and ethical operations. Some key aspects of ethical business practices include:

1. Corporate Governance and Ethics: Businesses will prioritize strong corporate governance structures that promote ethical decision-making and accountability. They will establish codes of conduct that guide employee behavior and ensure compliance with legal, social, and environmental standards.

2. Stakeholder Engagement: Ethical businesses will actively engage with stakeholders, including employees, customers, communities, and investors, to understand their needs and concerns. This engagement will facilitate the development of strategies that balance profitability with social and environmental responsibility.

3. Employee Well-being: Ethical businesses will prioritize the well-being of their employees, ensuring fair wages, safe working conditions, and opportunities for growth and development. They will foster inclusive and diverse workplaces, valuing employee well-being as a key driver of organizational success.

4. Innovation for Sustainability: Ethical businesses will invest in research and development to drive sustainable innovation. They will develop eco-friendly products, implement circular economy practices, and explore renewable energy solutions. Collaboration and knowledge-sharing across industries will be crucial in addressing global sustainability challenges.

5. Philanthropy and Social Impact: Ethical businesses will actively contribute to social and environmental causes. They will allocate resources to philanthropic initiatives, engage in volunteer activities, and support

community development projects. This commitment to social impact will go beyond mere token gestures, creating tangible benefits for society.

Conscious consumerism and ethical business practices are essential pillars of a sustainable economy in 2100. By embracing conscious consumerism, individuals will wield their purchasing power to drive positive change and reward businesses that prioritize sustainability and ethics. In turn, businesses will adopt transparent and responsible practices, recognizing that long-term success hinges on meeting consumer expectations. Together, conscious consumers and ethical businesses will shape a future where economic prosperity is intricately woven with social and environmental well-being.

Sustainable living and green innovations are at the forefront of societal trans-formation in 2100. The integration of renewable energy, smart cities, circular economy principles, sustainable food systems, eco-friendly transportation, nature-inspired innovations, and conscious consumerism has paved the path towards a resilient and regenerative future. By embracing these practices and supporting green innovations, we can create a world where ecological balance and human well-being go hand in hand, ensuring a sustainable legacy for generations to come.

8

Preserving Biodiversity in a Changing World

Preserving Biodiversity in a Changing World in 2100: A Call to Action for a Sustainable Future

Introduction:

In the year 2100, the world will face unprecedented challenges in preserving biodiversity. The Earth's ecosystems will continue to be threatened by climate change, habitat loss, pollution, and other human activities. However, recognizing the critical importance of biodiversity for the well-being of our planet and future generations, concerted efforts will be made to protect and restore the richness of life on Earth. This article explores the urgent need for preserving biodiversity in a changing world and highlights key strategies for ensuring a sustainable future.

The Importance of Biodiversity:

Biodiversity is the web of life that encompasses all living organisms on Earth and the intricate relationships between them. It provides numerous ecosystem services, including food production, clean air and water, climate regulation, and disease control. Biodiversity also holds immense cultural, aesthetic, and spiritual value, enriching our lives in profound ways. However, the loss of biodiversity threatens these invaluable benefits and disrupts the delicate balance of ecosystems.

Challenges to Biodiversity Conservation in 2100:

1. Climate Change: Rising temperatures, extreme weather events, and changing rainfall patterns will pose significant challenges to biodiversity. Species may struggle to adapt or migrate fast enough to new habitats, leading to range contractions or even extinction.
2. Habitat Loss and Fragmentation: Human activities such as deforestation, urbanization, and agriculture continue to degrade and fragment natural habitats, diminishing biodiversity hotspots and disrupting ecological connectivity.
3. Pollution and Contamination: Pollution from industries, agriculture, and improper waste disposal poses a significant threat to biodiversity. Chemical pollutants, including pesticides and plastics, can accumulate in ecosystems, impacting species survival and reproductive success.
4. Invasive Species: The introduction of non-native species can outcompete and displace native species, altering ecosystem dynamics and reducing biodiversity. Invasive species can also introduce new diseases and disrupt ecological interactions.

Preservation Strategies for Biodiversity:

1. Protected Areas and Conservation Reserves: Establishing and expanding protected areas will be crucial for preserving biodiversity in 2100. These areas provide safe havens for species and ecosystems, allowing them to recover and thrive. It is essential to ensure effective management, enforcement, and connectivity between protected areas.
2. Habitat Restoration and Connectivity: Restoring degraded habitats and creating ecological corridors will facilitate the movement of species, promote genetic diversity, and enhance ecosystem resilience. Habitat restoration efforts should prioritize native species and ecosystem functionality.
3. Sustainable Land and Resource Use: Adopting sustainable land-use practices, such as agroforestry, sustainable forestry, and regenerative

agriculture, will minimize the impact on natural habitats and support biodiversity conservation. Responsible resource extraction and mining practices should be implemented, considering biodiversity protection as a priority.

4. Collaboration and International Cooperation: Preserving biodiversity requires collective action and international cooperation. Governments, NGOs, scientific communities, and local communities should work together to develop effective conservation strategies, share knowledge and resources, and promote sustainable development practices.

5. Public Awareness and Education: Raising awareness about the importance of biodiversity and its connection to human well-being is vital. Education initiatives should emphasize the value of biodiversity, the impact of human activities, and individual actions that can contribute to its conservation. Engaging communities in conservation efforts fosters a sense of ownership and stewardship.

6. Sustainable Development Goals Integration: Biodiversity conservation should be integrated into broader sustainable development goals, such as poverty eradication, climate action, and sustainable consumption and production. This ensures that biodiversity conservation becomes a central aspect of global agendas.

In 2100, preserving biodiversity will be a critical challenge in the face of a changing world. However, it is a challenge that we must embrace with determination and urgency. By recognizing the importance of biodiversity, adopting sustainable practices, and working collaboratively, we can protect and restore the intricate web of life on Earth. Preserving biodiversity is not just an ethical imperative; it is essential for our survival and the well-being of future generations. Let us take action now to ensure a sustainable and biodiverse planet for all.

IV

Advancements in Space Exploration

9

Colonizing New Worlds

In the year 2100, humanity will embark on an extraordinary endeavor – the colonization of new worlds beyond Earth. With advancements in space exploration, technology, and our understanding of the universe, humans will venture into the vast expanse of space to establish settlements on distant planets and moons. This article explores the possibilities and challenges of colonizing new worlds in 2100 and envisions a future where humanity expands its horizons beyond our home planet.

The Imperative for Space Colonization:

1. Population Growth and Limited Resources: Earth's population will continue to grow, placing immense pressure on limited resources. Space colonization offers the potential for access to new sources of energy, minerals, and raw materials that can sustain our expanding civilization.

2. Planetary Resilience: Establishing colonies on other worlds is a vital step towards ensuring the long-term survival of humanity. By populating multiple planets, we can mitigate the risks of natural disasters, pandemics, and other catastrophic events that may threaten life on Earth.

3. Scientific Exploration and Knowledge: Colonizing new worlds will enable us to conduct groundbreaking scientific research, unlocking mysteries of the universe, and expanding our understanding of life,

evolution, and the origins of the cosmos.

Challenges and Opportunities:

1. Interplanetary Travel and Infrastructure: The distance and travel time involved in reaching new worlds pose significant challenges. Developing advanced propulsion systems, space habitats, and infrastructure will be crucial for successful colonization missions.
2. Environmental Adaptation: New worlds have vastly different environments, with unique atmospheric compositions, gravity levels, and geological features. Adapting to these environments and developing sustainable life-support systems will be essential for long-term habitation.
3. Self-Sufficiency and Resource Management: Colonies will need to be self-sufficient, relying on local resources for sustenance, energy production, and manufacturing. Advanced technologies such as 3D printing and closed-loop recycling systems will play a vital role in resource management.
4. Health and Well-being: Maintaining the physical and mental health of colonists in the isolated and harsh environments of new worlds will be a priority. Advanced medical technologies, psychological support systems, and recreational facilities will contribute to their well-being and overall success.
5. Ethical Considerations: The colonization of new worlds raises ethical questions regarding the preservation of indigenous life forms and the responsible stewardship of extraterrestrial environments. Balancing human exploration with respect for the ecosystems we encounter will be crucial.

Collaboration and International Cooperation:

Colonizing new worlds will require unprecedented levels of collaboration and international cooperation. Governments, space agencies, private companies, and scientific institutions must work together to pool resources, share knowledge, and coordinate efforts. International agreements and protocols will be necessary to govern exploration, settlement, and the responsible use of extraterrestrial resources.

As we embark on this ambitious journey, we must recognize that the challenges ahead are immense, and no single entity can accomplish them alone. It is through collaboration and international cooperation that we can harness our collective knowledge, resources, and expertise to pave the way for a new era of human exploration and settlement.

The colonization of new worlds, whether it be the moon, Mars, or beyond, requires a concerted effort involving governments, space agencies, private companies, and scientific institutions from around the globe. The complexity and scale of such an endeavor demand that we pool our resources, share our knowledge, and coordinate our efforts to maximize efficiency and ensure the success of our mission.

First and foremost, collaboration allows us to leverage the strengths of different nations and organizations. Each entity brings unique capabilities, expertise, and perspectives to the table. By working together, we can combine our strengths, fill in gaps, and overcome challenges that would be insurmountable if we were to go it alone. Through collaboration, we can accelerate technological advancements, streamline research, and optimize our utilization of resources.

International cooperation is equally crucial in shaping the framework for space exploration and colonization. Establishing international agreements and protocols is essential to govern exploration, settlement, and the responsible use of extraterrestrial resources. We must develop guidelines that promote fairness, sustainability, and the preservation of celestial bodies' inherent value. These agreements will foster trust, prevent conflicts, and ensure that the benefits of space exploration are shared equitably among nations.

Furthermore, collaboration and international cooperation in space exploration can serve as a blueprint for broader global cooperation on Earth. The challenges we face in colonizing new worlds demand a level of unity and cooperation that transcends national boundaries and political differences.

By working together towards a common goal, we can foster a spirit of understanding, goodwill, and mutual respect that extends beyond our endeavors in space.

However, collaboration and international cooperation are not without their challenges. Differences in cultural norms, geopolitical tensions, and conflicting interests may pose obstacles along the way. But it is precisely in the face of these challenges that the true strength of collaboration and international cooperation shines through. By engaging in open dialogue, forging partnerships, and finding common ground, we can overcome these hurdles and pave the way for a brighter future.

The quest to colonize new worlds is not solely about expanding human presence into the cosmos. It is also an opportunity to unite as a global community, transcending our differences and working together towards a shared vision. It is a chance to demonstrate our capacity for collaboration, innovation, and problem-solving on a global scale.

In conclusion, let us embrace the power of collaboration and international cooperation as we embark on the journey to colonize new worlds. Let us recognize that by coming together, we can achieve far more than we ever could alone. Through collaboration, we can push the boundaries of human exploration, unlock new frontiers of knowledge, and inspire generations to come. Together, we can forge a future where the wonders of the universe are within reach for all of humanity.

The colonization of new worlds in 2100 represents a pivotal moment in human history. It offers the potential for boundless scientific discoveries, resource utilization, and the expansion of our species into the cosmos. However, it also presents immense challenges that require careful planning, technological advancements, and a strong ethical framework. As we venture into the unknown, let us remember the responsibility to act as responsible stewards of the universe, ensuring the preservation of its wonders while pursuing the potential for human progress.

10

Interplanetary Travel and Beyond

In the year 2100, humanity will push the boundaries of space exploration further than ever before. Interplanetary travel, once a distant dream, will become a reality as we set our sights on exploring and colonizing new worlds. This article delves into the exciting prospects of interplanetary travel and envisions a future where humanity ventures beyond our solar system, unlocking the mysteries of the universe.

Advancements in Interplanetary Travel:

1. Propulsion Systems: Breakthroughs in propulsion technology will revolutionize interplanetary travel. From ion drives to nuclear propulsion, these systems will propel spacecraft with unprecedented speed, allowing us to reach distant planets in a matter of months or even weeks.

2. Sustainable Energy: The development of sustainable energy sources, such as advanced solar panels and nuclear fusion, will provide the necessary power for long-duration space missions. This sustainable energy will ensure self-sufficiency and reduce our reliance on Earth-based resources.

3. Advanced Life-Support Systems: The creation of sophisticated life-support systems will enable astronauts to survive and thrive during extended journeys. Closed-loop recycling systems, advanced hydroponics, and regenerative medicine will sustain human life in the inhospitable

environment of space.

Colonizing New Worlds:

1. Mars Colonization: Mars, the closest habitable planet to Earth, will be the primary target for colonization. With the establishment of sustainable habitats, humans will begin building self-sufficient colonies, laying the groundwork for future interplanetary civilizations.
2. Lunar Outposts: The Moon will serve as a stepping stone for deeper space exploration. Lunar outposts will serve as research stations and resource extraction sites, providing valuable insights and materials for interplanetary missions.
3. Asteroid Mining: The abundance of resources found within asteroids will fuel the expansion of space exploration. Mining operations will extract precious metals, water, and other vital resources needed for sustaining interplanetary colonies and supporting Earth's growing population.

Beyond Our Solar System:

I invite you to embark on a journey that transcends the boundaries of our solar system. Let us venture into the realm of the unknown and explore the possibilities that lie beyond the stars. In the coming decades, breakthroughs in space exploration technology will pave the way for humanity to reach out to distant star systems, and today, I present to you three fascinating concepts that will shape the future of interstellar exploration.

The first concept is interstellar probes. With advancements in propulsion technology, we will witness the launch of unmanned spacecraft capable of traversing the vast expanse of space and reaching other star systems. These interstellar probes will be our eyes and ears, carrying a wealth of scientific instruments to gather data about exoplanets, their atmospheres, and potential signs of extraterrestrial life. Imagine the wealth of knowledge we will acquire as these probes venture into the great unknown, unveiling the secrets of distant worlds and expanding our understanding of the universe.

The second concept is generation ships. As we set our sights on interstellar travel, the idea of self-sustaining spacecraft designed to carry multiple generations of humans becomes a reality. These generation ships will be marvels of engineering, equipped with advanced ecosystems, renewable resources, and artificial gravity to ensure the survival and well-being of the crew during the long and arduous journey. Generations will be born, live, and pass on, as humanity pushes the boundaries of exploration, all while maintaining a self-sufficient and thriving community aboard these cosmic vessels. It is a testament to our resilience and determination to venture into the unknown, knowing that the legacy we leave behind will be carried forward by those who come after us.

The third concept is wormhole exploration. The theoretical existence of wormholes, shortcuts through space-time, has captivated the imaginations of scientists and science fiction enthusiasts alike. In the years to come, we may unlock the secrets of these cosmic gateways, enabling near-instantaneous travel between distant regions of the universe. Wormhole exploration holds the promise of unprecedented interstellar connectivity, allowing us to traverse vast cosmic distances in a fraction of the time it would otherwise take. The potential for interstellar trade, cultural exchange, and the expansion of our collective knowledge becomes boundless as we harness the power of these cosmic conduits.

As we embark on this extraordinary journey, let us remember the significance of what lies ahead. Beyond our solar system lies a tapestry of unexplored worlds, waiting for us to unravel their mysteries. The pursuit of interstellar exploration is not merely a scientific endeavor; it is an embodiment of our innate curiosity, our insatiable thirst for knowledge, and our boundless spirit of discovery.

However, we must approach these endeavors with responsibility and mindfulness. As we venture into uncharted territories, we must do so with respect for the worlds we encounter, ensuring that we preserve the sanctity of life and the delicate balance of ecosystems. It is our duty to be stewards of the universe, preserving its beauty and diversity for future generations to cherish.

In conclusion, the future of space exploration extends far beyond our solar system. Interstellar probes will gather invaluable data, generation ships will carry us to new frontiers, and wormhole exploration may revolutionize our understanding of distance and time. Let us embrace these concepts with open minds and open hearts, for it is through our collective efforts that we will unravel the mysteries of the cosmos and forge a path toward a future where the stars are no longer beyond our reach.

1. Interstellar Probes: Breakthroughs in propulsion technology will enable the launch of interstellar probes, unmanned spacecraft capable of exploring other star systems. These probes will provide valuable data about exoplanets, their atmospheres, and potential signs of extraterrestrial life.

2. Generation Ships: The concept of generation ships, self-sustaining spacecraft designed to carry multiple generations of humans to distant star systems, will become a reality. These vessels will be equipped with advanced ecosystems, renewable resources, and artificial gravity, ensuring the survival of the crew during the long journey.

3. Wormhole Exploration: The discovery and understanding of wormholes, theoretical shortcuts through space-time, may unlock the potential for near-instantaneous travel between distant regions of the universe. This revolutionary technology could open up a new era of interstellar exploration.

Interplanetary travel and exploration in 2100 will mark a new chapter in human history. It will not only expand our knowledge of the cosmos but also offer solutions to challenges on Earth, such as resource scarcity and environmental sustainability. As we set our sights on the stars, let us embrace the spirit of curiosity, collaboration, and responsible stewardship of the universe. Interplanetary travel and beyond hold the promise of a future where humanity reaches new frontiers, unravels the mysteries of the universe, and secures our place among the stars.

V

Future of Medicine and Healthcare

11

Medical Breakthroughs and Longevity

As we peer into the future, the year 2100 holds immense potential for medical breakthroughs that could revolutionize healthcare and greatly impact human longevity. With rapid advancements in technology, genetics, regenerative medicine, and artificial intelligence, the boundaries of what is possible in healthcare are expanding. This chapter explores speculative yet fascinating possibilities of medical breakthroughs that could transform human health and extend lifespan in the year 2100.

1.Genomic Editing and Customized Medicine:

By 2100, genomic editing technologies may have reached unprecedented heights, allowing precise modifications to an individual's genetic code. CRISPR-Cas9 and other gene editing tools could be routinely used to correct disease-causing mutations, eradicate hereditary disorders, and enhance overall health. Customized medicine may become the norm, with treatments tailored to an individual's unique genetic makeup, optimizing therapeutic outcomes and preventing diseases before they manifest.

The year 2100 holds remarkable promise for medical advancements, and one area that is set to revolutionize healthcare is genomic editing and customized medicine. Building upon the foundation laid by CRISPR-Cas9 and other gene editing technologies, the future may witness unprecedented precision in modifying the human genome. This essay explores the potential implications and ethical considerations surrounding genomic editing and the advent of customized medicine in 2100.

- **Precision Genome Editing**: By 2100, genomic editing technologies are likely to have advanced to an extraordinary degree. Highly refined and precise tools could enable scientists and healthcare professionals to edit specific genes with unparalleled accuracy. The ability to correct disease-causing mutations at the molecular level could transform the treatment of genetic disorders and inherited conditions. Diseases that were once considered incurable may become manageable or even eradicated.
- **Personalized Therapies:** Customized medicine based on an individual's genetic makeup is poised to become the cornerstone of healthcare in 2100. Comprehensive genomic profiling and analysis could provide insights into an individual's genetic predispositions, allowing healthcare providers to develop tailored treatment plans. Medications could be designed specifically to target a person's genetic variants, maximizing therapeutic efficacy and minimizing adverse effects. Personalized therapies may extend beyond pharmacology, encompassing lifestyle interventions, dietary recommendations, and preventive measures.
- **Disease Prevention and Prediction:** Genomic editing in conjunction with advanced predictive analytics could revolutionize disease prevention strategies. By identifying individuals at high risk of developing certain conditions, healthcare providers could implement preemptive measures to mitigate disease onset. Genome sequencing early in life could provide a comprehensive genetic blueprint, enabling proactive interventions and personalized health monitoring throughout an individual's lifespan.
- **Ethical Considerations:** As the capabilities of genomic editing expand, ethical considerations become paramount. Striking a balance between the potential benefits and the ethical boundaries is crucial. Questions surrounding genetic enhancement, germline editing, and equitable access to customized medicine will require careful examination. Strict ethical frameworks, transparent guidelines, and robust regulatory mechanisms must be in place to ensure responsible and equitable implementation of genomic editing technologies.

- **Socioeconomic Implications:** The widespread availability and affordability of genomic editing and customized medicine may give rise to socioeconomic disparities. Access to these cutting-edge technologies could be limited to those with financial means, exacerbating existing healthcare inequalities. It is imperative that governments, policymakers, and healthcare systems work collectively to ensure equitable access and prioritize the needs of underserved populations.
- **Public Perception and Education:** Effective communication and education will be pivotal in shaping public perception and acceptance of genomic editing. Open dialogue, transparent information sharing, and comprehensive education programs can help dispel misconceptions, address concerns, and foster a responsible and informed approach towards genomic editing and customized medicine.

Genomic editing and customized medicine have the potential to redefine healthcare in 2100, providing unprecedented opportunities to address genetic disorders, prevent diseases, and optimize treatment outcomes. However, as we venture into this future, ethical considerations, equitable access, and responsible implementation must be at the forefront. By navigating these challenges with careful deliberation and societal consensus, we can harness the power of genomic editing to improve human health, extend lifespans, and usher in a new era of personalized medicine that benefits all of humanity.

2.Nanotechnology and Cellular Repair:

Nanotechnology holds tremendous potential in the future of medicine. Miniature nanobots could be deployed within the human body, precisely targeting damaged cells, organs, or tissues. These nanobots could repair cellular structures, eliminate cancerous growths, and restore organ functionality. Furthermore, nanomaterials could be used to develop advanced drug delivery systems, ensuring targeted and efficient administration of medications.

Advancements in nanotechnology have the potential to revolutionize healthcare in the future, particularly in the field of cellular repair. By the year 2100, nanotechnology is expected to have progressed significantly, enabling precise manipulation and healing of cells at the microscopic level. This essay explores the potential implications and transformative effects of nanotechnology in cellular repair in the year 2100.

- **Targeted Cell Repair:** In 2100, nanobots and nanoscale devices may be routinely employed for targeted cell repair. These microscopic machines could be designed to identify damaged or dysfunctional cells and apply therapeutic interventions directly at the cellular level. Nanobots equipped with specific sensors and drug delivery systems could accurately locate and repair damaged DNA, restore cellular functions, and reverse the effects of various diseases.

- **Cancer Treatment and Elimination:** Nanotechnology could play a pivotal role in the fight against cancer in 2100. Nanoparticles designed to selectively target cancer cells could deliver therapeutic agents directly to tumors, minimizing damage to healthy tissue. Advanced nanodevices may be capable of detecting early-stage cancer cells, allowing for precise and timely intervention. Additionally, nanobots could be programmed to identify and eliminate circulating tumor cells, preventing metastasis and significantly improving cancer treatment outcomes.

- **Regeneration and Tissue Engineering:** In the future, nanotechnology could enable breakthroughs in tissue regeneration and engineering. Nanoscale scaffolds and materials could be used to stimulate and guide the growth of new tissue, facilitating the regeneration of damaged or lost organs. By combining nanotechnology with stem cell research, scientists may be able to create functional organs in the laboratory, ready for transplantation. This approach could alleviate organ shortages, eliminate the need for immunosuppressant drugs, and enhance the success rates of organ transplants.

- **Drug Delivery Systems:** Nanotechnology offers the potential for highly efficient and targeted drug delivery systems. Nanoparticles carrying therapeutic agents could be engineered to release medications at specific sites within the body, improving drug efficacy while minimizing side effects. Nano-sized devices could also provide controlled and sustained release of drugs, reducing the frequency of administration and enhancing patient compliance. Moreover, nanosensors incorporated into drug delivery systems could monitor treatment responses in real-time, enabling personalized adjustments to therapy.

- **Biomedical Imaging:** Nanotechnology-based imaging techniques could revolutionize diagnostics in 2100. Highly sensitive nanosensors and contrast agents could provide detailed and real-time imaging of cells, tissues, and even individual molecules. This enhanced imaging capability could facilitate early detection of diseases, precise targeting of treatment areas, and monitoring of therapeutic responses. Nanoscale imaging devices may also enable non-invasive, high-resolution imaging of the brain, leading to advancements in understanding and treating neurological disorders.

- **Ethical Considerations and Safety:** As nanotechnology evolves, it is crucial to address ethical considerations and safety concerns. Robust regulations and guidelines should be in place to ensure the responsible development and deployment of nanotechnology in healthcare. Thorough testing for potential toxicity and long-term effects should be conducted to ensure the safety of nanomaterials and nanodevices.

Nanotechnology holds immense potential for cellular repair and medical advancements in the year 2100. From targeted cell repair and cancer treatment to tissue regeneration and drug delivery systems, the microscopic capabilities of nanotechnology can reshape the landscape of healthcare. However, ethical considerations, safety protocols, and equitable access to nanotechnology-based therapies must be carefully addressed. With responsible implementation, nanotechnology can unlock new frontiers in cellular repair, improving health outcomes and offering new hope for patients worldwide.

3.Regenerative Medicine and Tissue Engineering:

The field of regenerative medicine is expected to make significant strides by 2100. Stem cell research and tissue engineering techniques may enable the creation of functional organs and tissues in the laboratory, ready for transplantation. Advanced 3D bioprinting could allow for the fabrication of personalized organs, reducing the waiting time for organ transplants and eliminating the need for immunosuppressant drugs.

Regenerative medicine and tissue engineering have the potential to transform healthcare in the future, particularly in the field of organ regeneration. By the year 2100, advancements in these fields may revolutionize the way we approach organ failure and transplantation. This essay explores the potential implications and transformative effects of regenerative medicine and tissue engineering in 2100.

- **Organ Regeneration:** In 2100, regenerative medicine could enable the regeneration of functional organs using a combination of stem cells, scaffolds, and growth factors. Scientists may be able to create bioengineered organs in the laboratory, mimicking the complexity and functionality of natural organs. These engineered organs could provide a limitless supply for transplantation, eliminating the need for organ waiting lists and reducing the risks associated with organ rejection.
- **3D Bioprinting**: By 2100, 3D bioprinting may have advanced to a level where the precise fabrication of complex tissues and organs becomes a reality. Using specialized bioinks containing living cells, bioprinters could create intricately designed structures layer by layer, replicating the architecture and functionality of native tissues. This technology could be employed to generate patient-specific organs, reducing the risk of rejection and improving transplantation success rates.
- **Tissue Regeneration:** Regenerative medicine could also facilitate the repair and regeneration of damaged tissues throughout the body. By harnessing the regenerative potential of stem cells and employing tissue engineering techniques, scientists may be able to stimulate the regeneration of injured or degenerated tissues, such as cartilage, spinal

cord, and cardiac muscle. This approach could offer new treatment options for conditions that currently have limited therapeutic solutions.

- **Biomaterials and Scaffolds:** In 2100, advancements in biomaterials and scaffolds may play a crucial role in tissue engineering. These materials could provide a supportive structure for cells to grow, differentiate, and organize into functional tissues and organs. Biomaterials with enhanced biocompatibility and bioactivity could promote cellular adhesion, migration, and integration, facilitating the regeneration process. Tailored scaffolds could also provide mechanical support and guide the formation of complex tissue architectures.

- **Stem Cell Therapies:** Stem cell therapies may become more advanced and widely available in 2100. With a deeper understanding of stem cell biology and the development of innovative techniques, scientists could harness the potential of different types of stem cells, including induced pluripotent stem cells (iPSCs) and adult stem cells, for tissue regeneration and organ repair. Stem cell-based therapies could provide personalized treatments for various conditions, promoting healing and functional restoration.

- **Ethical Considerations and Safety:** The progress of regenerative medicine and tissue engineering in 2100 must be accompanied by careful consideration of ethical and safety issues. Ensuring the responsible use of stem cells, addressing concerns related to genetic modification, and maintaining stringent safety standards will be imperative. Ethical frameworks and regulations should guide the development and application of these technologies to ensure that they are used in a manner that benefits individuals and society as a whole.

Regenerative medicine and tissue engineering hold immense promise for organ regeneration and tissue repair in 2100. The ability to create bioengineered organs, regenerate damaged tissues, and employ advanced 3D bioprinting techniques could transform healthcare, offering new solutions for organ failure and tissue damage. However, ethical considerations, safety protocols, and equitable access to these therapies must be carefully addressed to ensure their responsible implementation. With continued advancements and responsible practices, regenerative medicine and tissue engineering have the potential to revolutionize healthcare, enhancing quality of life and offering new hope to patients in need.

4.Artificial Intelligence in Healthcare:

Artificial intelligence (AI) will likely play a pivotal role in healthcare by 2100. AI algorithms could analyze vast amounts of medical data to identify patterns, predict diseases, and recommend tailored treatment plans. Machine learning algorithms may assist in drug discovery, accelerating the development of new therapeutics. AI-powered robotic assistants could support healthcare professionals in surgery, diagnosis, and patient care, improving precision and efficiency.

Artificial intelligence (AI) has already made significant strides in healthcare, but by the year 2100, it is expected to reach unparalleled levels of sophistication and integration. AI has the potential to revolutionize healthcare systems, augment medical professionals' capabilities, and improve patient outcomes. This essay explores the potential implications and transformative effects of AI in healthcare in the year 2100.

- **Precision Diagnosis and Predictive Analytics:** In 2100, AI algorithms could provide precise and timely diagnoses by analyzing vast amounts of patient data, including medical records, imaging results, and genetic profiles. Machine learning algorithms could identify patterns and indicators that humans might overlook, leading to earlier detection of diseases and more accurate prognoses. AI-powered predictive analytics may enable the identification of individuals at high risk of developing specific conditions, allowing for preventive interventions and personalized healthcare plans.
- **AI-assisted Treatment Planning:** In the future, AI could assist health-

care providers in developing customized treatment plans for patients. By analyzing individual patient data, including genetics, medical history, and real-time monitoring, AI algorithms could recommend optimal treatment options, dosage adjustments, and medication combinations. AI could help optimize treatment outcomes, reduce adverse effects, and improve patient adherence to treatment regimens.

- **Robotics and Surgical Assistance:** By 2100, surgical procedures could be significantly enhanced by AI-powered robotics. Surgeons may work alongside robotic assistants that can perform precise and complex tasks, such as suturing, tissue manipulation, and delicate maneuvers. AI algorithms could analyze real-time patient data during surgery, providing surgeons with augmented insights and guidance for optimal decision-making. This combination of human expertise and AI assistance could enhance surgical precision and efficiency.

- **Intelligent Healthcare Systems:** AI could transform healthcare systems by creating intelligent, interconnected networks. In 2100, AI-powered systems could seamlessly integrate patient data from various sources, facilitating comprehensive and real-time patient monitoring. AI algorithms may identify potential treatment interactions, monitor vital signs, and trigger alerts for immediate medical attention. Intelligent systems could also streamline administrative tasks, improve resource allocation, and enhance overall operational efficiency.

- **Personalized Medicine and Drug Discovery:** In 2100, AI could enable truly personalized medicine by analyzing individual patient data to predict treatment responses and recommend tailored therapies. AI algorithms could match patients with the most effective medications based on their genetic profiles, disease characteristics, and response patterns. Furthermore, AI-powered drug discovery platforms could accelerate the development of novel therapeutics by simulating drug interactions, predicting efficacy, and identifying potential side effects.

- **Ethical Considerations and Data Privacy:** As AI becomes increasingly integrated into healthcare, ethical considerations and data privacy become paramount. Striking a balance between data utilization for improved patient care and safeguarding individual privacy will be crucial. Robust regulations, transparent data governance, and responsible AI development practices should be in place to ensure patient confidentiality, informed consent, and equitable access to AI-driven healthcare technologies.

AI in healthcare has the potential to transform diagnosis, treatment, and patient care in 2100. From precision diagnosis and predictive analytics to AI-assisted treatment planning and robotic surgical assistance, the possibilities are vast. By leveraging the power of AI, healthcare systems can become more efficient, accurate, and patient-centered. However, ethical considerations, data privacy, and responsible AI deployment must be at the forefront of these advancements. With a careful balance of technological progress and ethical frameworks, AI has the potential to revolutionize healthcare, improving patient outcomes and fostering a new era of personalized and efficient healthcare in the future.

5.Longevity Therapies and Age Reversal:

Advancements in understanding the biology of aging may lead to the development of therapies aimed at extending human lifespan and promoting healthy aging. Telomere extension, senescence reversal, and epigenetic reprogramming techniques could potentially rejuvenate cells and tissues, slowing down the aging process. Combining these therapies with personalized lifestyle interventions may significantly increase human lifespan and improve overall well-being.

The quest for longevity and age reversal has captivated human imagination for centuries. In the year 2100, advancements in biomedical research and emerging technologies may bring us closer to realizing the dream of prolonged youthfulness and extended lifespans. This essay explores the potential implications and transformative effects of longevity therapies and age reversal in the year 2100.

- **Telomere Extension and Cellular Regeneration:** In 2100, breakthroughs in telomere extension and cellular regeneration could unlock new possibilities for slowing down the aging process. Telomeres, the protective caps at the ends of chromosomes, play a crucial role in cellular aging. By developing interventions that extend telomere length, scientists may be able to delay cellular senescence and promote cellular rejuvenation. This could lead to improved tissue function, enhanced organ health, and extended healthy lifespan.
- **Genetic and Epigenetic Interventions:** Advancements in genetic and epigenetic therapies could enable targeted interventions for age-related diseases and age-associated decline. Gene editing technologies, such as CRISPR-Cas9, may be refined to correct genetic mutations linked to aging and age-related disorders. Epigenetic modifications could be employed to reverse age-associated changes in gene expression, restoring youthful cellular states. These interventions could potentially slow down the aging process and rejuvenate tissues and organs.
- **Stem Cell Therapies and Tissue Engineering:** In 2100, stem cell therapies and tissue engineering approaches may play a vital role in age reversal. Stem cells, with their regenerative potential, could be harnessed to repair and replace damaged or aging cells and tissues. By combining stem cell therapies with tissue engineering techniques, scientists may be able to regenerate functional organs and tissues, rejuvenating the body and restoring youthful vitality.
- **Pharmacological Interventions:** Pharmacological interventions tailored to age reversal could become a reality in 2100. Anti-aging drugs, also known as geroprotectors, may be developed to target specific aging pathways and slow down the biological aging process. These drugs could mitigate age-related diseases, improve cellular function, and promote overall health and longevity. Combination therapies that target multiple aging mechanisms could provide synergistic effects, enhancing their effectiveness.

- **Personalized Aging Interventions:** Advancements in personalized medicine could extend to personalized aging interventions in 2100. With a comprehensive understanding of an individual's genetic makeup, epigenetic profile, and health data, tailored interventions could be designed to address specific aging-related factors and optimize healthspan. Personalized lifestyle interventions, including dietary recommendations, exercise plans, and stress management strategies, could be integrated with medical interventions to promote healthy aging and extend lifespan.
- **Ethical Considerations and Societal Implications:** The pursuit of longevity and age reversal raises important ethical considerations. Questions surrounding equitable access to these therapies, the potential for exacerbating societal inequalities, and the psychological and social impact of significantly extended lifespans must be carefully addressed. Ethical frameworks, societal dialogue, and regulatory oversight will be critical in ensuring responsible and equitable implementation of longevity therapies.

Longevity therapies and age reversal have the potential to transform human aging and extend healthy lifespan in 2100. Telomere extension, genetic and epigenetic interventions, stem cell therapies, tissue engineering, and pharmacological interventions may collectively contribute to a future where age-related diseases are delayed or reversed, and human vitality is rejuvenated. However, ethical considerations, equitable access, and responsible implementation should guide the development and deployment of these therapies. By leveraging advancements in science and technology responsibly, we can aspire to a future where healthy aging and extended lifespans enhance the quality of life for individuals and society as a whole.

While the future remains uncertain, the potential medical breakthroughs and advancements discussed in this chapter offer glimpses into a transformed healthcare landscape in 2100. From precision medicine tailored to individual genetic profiles to nanotechnology repairing cells at a microscopic level, and from regenerative medicine creating organs in the lab to AI-powered healthcare systems, the possibilities are awe-inspiring. As we embark on this journey towards a healthier future, ethical considerations and responsible implementation of these technologies will be vital to ensure their benefits are accessible to all, ultimately transforming human health and longevity in the years to come.

12

Revolutionizing Healthcare Delivery

Healthcare delivery has evolved significantly over the years, and by the year 2100, advancements in technology and innovative approaches are expected to revolutionize the way healthcare services are delivered. This chapter explores the potential implications and transformative effects of healthcare delivery in the year 2100, focusing on enhanced access to care, improved efficiency, and personalized patient-centered approaches.

1. **Telemedicine and Virtual Care:**

In 2100, telemedicine and virtual care will have become integral parts of healthcare delivery. Advanced communication technologies, virtual reality, and artificial intelligence (AI) will enable patients to connect with healthcare providers remotely, eliminating geographical barriers and enhancing access to care. Virtual consultations, remote monitoring, and telehealth platforms will enable timely and convenient healthcare interactions, especially for individuals in remote areas or with limited mobility.

The year 2100 presents a world where telemedicine and virtual care have become indispensable components of healthcare delivery. This chapter explores the transformative impact of advanced communication technologies, virtual reality, and artificial intelligence (AI) on healthcare, enabling remote patient-provider connections and revolutionizing the accessibility and convenience of care. It delves into the various applications and benefits of telemedicine in 2100, highlighting its potential to bridge geographical gaps, enhance patient outcomes, and reshape the healthcare landscape.

1. Evolution of Telemedicine: The chapter begins by tracing the evolution of telemedicine from its early beginnings to its advanced state in 2100. It explores the historical challenges and breakthroughs that paved the way for widespread adoption, including improvements in communication infrastructure, advancements in medical devices, and the integration of AI and virtual reality technologies.

2. Virtual Consultations and Remote Monitoring: In 2100, virtual consultations have become a standard mode of healthcare delivery. The chapter examines how patients can connect with healthcare providers from the comfort of their homes using advanced video conferencing and communication platforms. It explores the benefits of virtual consultations in reducing travel time, minimizing waiting periods, and improving access to specialized care. Additionally, the chapter explores remote monitoring technologies that enable healthcare providers to remotely monitor patients' vital signs and health status, facilitating proactive interventions and personalized care.

3. Telehealth Platforms and Accessibility: Telehealth platforms have revolutionized healthcare accessibility in 2100. The chapter delves into the features and functionalities of these platforms, which allow patients to access healthcare services, schedule appointments, receive medical advice, and access electronic health records remotely. It discusses the impact of telehealth platforms on reducing healthcare disparities, improving healthcare outcomes for underserved populations, and enhancing patient engagement.

4. Virtual Reality and Immersive Experiences: Virtual reality (VR) has transformed healthcare experiences in 2100. The chapter explores how VR technologies are used to create immersive healthcare environments, enabling patients to undergo virtual simulations, receive virtual therapy sessions, or engage in pain management techniques. It discusses the

potential of VR in enhancing patient comfort, reducing anxiety, and improving treatment adherence.

5. AI in Telemedicine: Artificial intelligence plays a vital role in telemedicine and virtual care in 2100. The chapter examines the applications of AI in areas such as triage systems, medical imaging analysis, and personalized treatment recommendations. It explores how AI-powered chatbots and virtual assistants provide patients with real-time medical advice, symptom assessment, and health information, improving healthcare accessibility and empowering individuals to make informed decisions.

6. Ethical and Legal Considerations: The chapter addresses the ethical and legal considerations that arise with the integration of telemedicine and virtual care in 2100. It explores issues of patient privacy, data security, consent, and the potential challenges of maintaining a humanistic approach in a digitally mediated healthcare environment. It emphasizes the importance of robust ethical frameworks and regulatory guidelines to ensure patient safety, privacy, and trust.

7. Future Directions and Challenges: The chapter concludes by discussing the future directions and challenges of telemedicine and virtual care in 2100. It explores the potential for further advancements in AI, virtual reality, and remote monitoring technologies. It also addresses challenges such as the digital divide, ensuring equitable access to telemedicine services, and integrating telemedicine seamlessly into existing healthcare systems.

Telemedicine and virtual care have revolutionized healthcare delivery in 2100, breaking down geographical barriers, enhancing access to care, and transforming the patient-provider relationship. The integration of advanced communication technologies, virtual reality, and AI has paved the way for personalized, convenient, and patient-centered healthcare experiences. While challenges and ethical considerations remain, embracing telemedicine and virtual care can lead to improved healthcare outcomes, enhanced patient satisfaction, and a more efficient and accessible healthcare system in the future.

2.AI-Driven Diagnostic and Decision Support Systems:

By 2100, AI-driven diagnostic and decision support systems will have transformed the diagnostic process. AI algorithms will analyze patient data, including medical records, imaging results, and genetic profiles, to provide accurate and efficient diagnoses. These systems will enhance the capabilities of healthcare professionals, assisting in complex decision-making, and improving diagnostic accuracy. AI will enable early detection of diseases, personalized treatment plans, and proactive preventive interventions.

AI-driven diagnostic and decision support systems. In the year 2100, these systems will have transformed the diagnostic process, reshaping the way we approach healthcare and improving patient outcomes.

Imagine a world where artificial intelligence algorithms are able to analyze vast amounts of patient data with unmatched precision and speed. Medical records, imaging results, genetic profiles, and even real-time patient monitoring data will all be seamlessly integrated and processed by these advanced AI systems. The result? Accurate and efficient diagnoses that were previously unimaginable.

One of the most significant benefits of AI-driven diagnostic systems is their ability to enhance the capabilities of healthcare professionals. These systems will serve as invaluable tools, assisting doctors in complex decision-making processes. By analyzing patient data and comparing it to vast databases of medical knowledge, AI algorithms will provide healthcare professionals with evidence-based insights and recommendations. This collaboration between human expertise and artificial intelligence will lead to more informed decisions and improved patient care.

Furthermore, AI-driven diagnostic systems will play a crucial role in early disease detection. By analyzing patterns and identifying subtle indicators, these systems will enable healthcare professionals to identify diseases in their earliest stages. This early detection will prove instrumental in improving treatment outcomes and saving lives. With AI support, medical professionals will be able to intervene before diseases progress, offering personalized treatment plans and maximizing the chances of successful recovery.

The potential of AI-driven diagnostic systems goes beyond individual patient care. These systems will contribute to population health by enabling proactive preventive interventions. By analyzing large datasets and identifying risk factors, AI algorithms will assist in identifying high-risk individuals and implementing preventive measures. This shift towards proactive healthcare will reduce the burden on healthcare systems and lead to improved public health outcomes.

However, as we embrace the possibilities offered by AI-driven diagnostic and decision support systems, we must also acknowledge the importance of ethical considerations and human oversight. While AI can provide valuable insights, the ultimate responsibility for patient care lies with healthcare professionals. Human judgment, empathy, and ethical decision-making must always be at the forefront, guiding the use of AI technologies in healthcare.

Additionally, ensuring the privacy and security of patient data is of paramount importance. As we entrust AI systems with sensitive medical information, robust safeguards must be in place to protect patient privacy and maintain confidentiality. Striking the right balance between data accessibility and privacy will be crucial in building trust and ensuring the responsible use of AI in healthcare.

In conclusion, AI-driven diagnostic and decision support systems are set to transform healthcare in 2100. These systems will enable accurate and efficient diagnoses, enhance the capabilities of healthcare professionals, facilitate early disease detection, and support proactive preventive interventions. As we embrace these advancements, let us do so with a steadfast commitment to ethics, privacy, and human-centered care. Together, we can harness the power of AI to create a future where healthcare is more precise, personalized, and accessible for all.

3.Robotics and Automation in Healthcare:

The integration of robotics and automation will reshape healthcare delivery in 2100. Robotic technologies will assist in surgeries, performing precise and delicate procedures under the guidance of human surgeons. Automation will streamline repetitive tasks, reducing the burden on healthcare professionals and minimizing errors. Robotic companions and assistants will provide support and care for patients, particularly the elderly or those with disabilities, improving their quality of life and overall healthcare experience.

In the year 2100, the integration of robotic technologies and automation will reshape healthcare delivery, offering unprecedented possibilities for patient care and medical advancements.

Imagine a future where surgical procedures are conducted with unmatched precision and efficiency, thanks to the assistance of robotic technologies. In the operating room, robotic surgical systems will work in tandem with human surgeons, performing delicate and complex procedures with unparalleled accuracy. These robotic systems will act as extensions of the surgeon's hands, enabling them to navigate intricate anatomical structures and manipulate surgical instruments with enhanced dexterity. The result? Safer, more precise surgeries, and improved patient outcomes.

Beyond the operating room, automation will play a pivotal role in streamlining healthcare processes. Repetitive tasks that currently consume significant time and resources will be delegated to automated systems. This will alleviate the burden on healthcare professionals, allowing them to focus on critical decision-making and providing personalized care. Automation will minimize the risk of human error, ensuring that routine tasks such as medication administration, data entry, and laboratory analysis are performed accurately and efficiently.

Robotics and automation will not only benefit healthcare professionals but will also enhance the patient experience. Robotic companions and assistants will provide support and care to patients, particularly those who are elderly or have disabilities. These robotic companions will assist with activities of daily living, monitor vital signs, and provide companionship and emotional support. They will also ensure that patients adhere to medication schedules and follow prescribed rehabilitation programs. The presence of these robotic companions will alleviate feelings of loneliness and improve the overall well-being of patients.

In addition to their physical assistance, robotics will contribute to medical advancements and research. Robotic systems will enable the collection and analysis of large datasets, aiding in the discovery of new treatments and therapies. They will also facilitate remote healthcare delivery, allowing patients to access specialized care regardless of their geographical location. This expanded access to medical expertise will improve healthcare equity and enhance patient outcomes worldwide.

As we embrace the integration of robotics and automation in healthcare, it is essential to address the ethical considerations that accompany these advancements. We must ensure that human oversight remains central to the decision-making process, with robotics and automation serving as tools to enhance human capabilities rather than replacing them. Ethical frameworks should guide the development and deployment of these technologies, emphasizing transparency, accountability, and patient-centered care.

Furthermore, it is crucial to acknowledge that robotics and automation should not lead to the dehumanization of healthcare. While technology can enhance efficiency and precision, the human touch and empathy remain integral to healthcare delivery. Maintaining a balance between technological advancements and compassionate care is essential to preserving the essence of medicine.

In conclusion, robotics and automation will revolutionize healthcare delivery in 2100. From assisting in surgeries to automating repetitive tasks, these technologies will enhance patient care, improve healthcare outcomes, and advance medical research. Robotic companions will provide support and care, enhancing the well-being of patients, while automation will streamline processes, allowing healthcare professionals to focus on personalized care. Let us embrace these advancements with a commitment to ethical considerations and human-centered healthcare. Together, we can shape a future where robotics and automation complement our expertise and compassion, creating a healthcare system that is both efficient and deeply caring.

4.Personalized Medicine and Genomic Healthcare:

In 2100, healthcare delivery will be increasingly personalized, driven by advances in genomics and precision medicine. Genomic profiling and analysis will guide treatment decisions, enabling tailored therapies based on an individual's genetic makeup and unique disease characteristics. Personalized medicine will optimize treatment efficacy, reduce adverse effects, and enhance patient outcomes. With the integration of wearable devices and real-time monitoring, healthcare providers will have access to continuous patient data, allowing for proactive interventions and personalized care plans.

In the year 2100, healthcare delivery will be revolutionized by the advancements in personalized medicine and genomic healthcare, transforming the way we prevent, diagnose, and treat diseases.

At the heart of this transformation lies the field of genomics. In 2100, the ability to sequence and analyze an individual's genome will be commonplace, allowing healthcare providers to gain a deep understanding of a person's genetic makeup and its implications on their health. Genomic profiling will serve as a powerful tool in guiding treatment decisions, enabling healthcare professionals to design tailored therapies that target the specific genetic drivers of a disease.

Personalized medicine will optimize treatment efficacy and minimize adverse effects. Gone will be the days of trial-and-error approaches, where patients may undergo treatments that are ineffective or cause unnecessary side effects. Instead, treatment plans will be tailored to each individual's genetic profile, ensuring that interventions are precisely matched to the unique characteristics of their disease. This approach will lead to improved patient outcomes and higher treatment success rates.

But personalized medicine goes beyond genetics. In 2100, wearable devices and real-time monitoring will become an integral part of healthcare delivery. These devices will continuously collect data on a patient's vital signs, activity levels, and even molecular biomarkers. This constant stream of information will empower healthcare providers to have a comprehensive and real-time understanding of their patients' health. It will enable proactive interventions, allowing healthcare professionals to detect early signs of deterioration or predict disease progression before it becomes symptomatic.

The integration of wearable devices and real-time monitoring will also pave the way for personalized care plans. With access to continuous patient data, healthcare providers will be able to fine-tune treatment regimens, adjusting medications or therapies in response to changes in the patient's health status. This personalized approach will ensure that patients receive the right treatment at the right time, leading to more effective interventions and improved patient outcomes.

However, as we embrace the promises of personalized medicine and genomic healthcare, we must also address the challenges that accompany these advancements. Privacy and data security will be of utmost importance in the era of genomics. Robust safeguards and ethical frameworks must be in place to protect patients' genetic information and ensure that it is used responsibly and with their informed consent.

Furthermore, it is crucial to ensure equitable access to personalized medicine. As the costs of genomic sequencing and personalized therapies decrease over time, efforts must be made to ensure that these innovations are accessible to all individuals, regardless of their socioeconomic status or geographic location. The democratization of personalized medicine will be essential in achieving healthcare equity and maximizing its impact on population health.

In conclusion, personalized medicine and genomic healthcare hold tremendous potential in transforming healthcare delivery in 2100. Through genomic profiling, tailored therapies, and real-time monitoring, we will witness a paradigm shift from a one-size-fits-all approach to precision medicine. The integration of wearable devices and continuous patient data will enable proactive interventions and personalized care plans. Let us embrace these advancements with a commitment to ethical considerations, data privacy, and equitable access. Together, we can create a future where healthcare is truly personalized, optimized, and focused on the individual needs of each patient.

5.Population Health Management and Preventive Care:

In 2100, healthcare delivery will place a strong emphasis on population health management and preventive care. Predictive analytics, AI algorithms, and big data will facilitate the identification of high-risk populations, enabling targeted preventive interventions and health promotion strategies. Public health campaigns, lifestyle interventions, and early detection programs will be implemented to prevent the onset of diseases and improve overall population health.

In the year 2100, healthcare delivery will be centered around proactive measures aimed at promoting the health and well-being of entire populations. Through the integration of predictive analytics, AI algorithms, and big data, healthcare providers will be able to identify high-risk populations and implement targeted interventions that will prevent the onset of diseases and improve overall population health.

In this future era, healthcare professionals will have access to vast amounts of data collected from various sources, including electronic health records, wearable devices, and population health databases. This wealth of information will be analyzed using advanced algorithms and predictive analytics to identify patterns and trends that can help anticipate health risks and identify high-risk populations. By harnessing the power of big data, healthcare providers will be able to proactively intervene and implement preventive strategies.

Preventive care will take center stage in healthcare delivery. Public health campaigns will be tailored to specific population groups, addressing their unique health challenges and promoting healthy behaviors. These campaigns will focus on raising awareness about the importance of a healthy lifestyle, including regular exercise, balanced nutrition, and stress management. By engaging individuals and communities, healthcare providers will empower them to take charge of their own health and make informed decisions that contribute to their well-being.

In addition to public health campaigns, lifestyle interventions will play a crucial role in preventive care. Personalized wellness programs will be developed, taking into account an individual's genetic predispositions, lifestyle factors, and environmental influences. These programs will provide tailored recommendations for diet, exercise, and stress reduction techniques. Through ongoing monitoring and support, individuals will be empowered to adopt healthy habits and reduce their risk of developing chronic diseases.

Early detection programs will also be a cornerstone of population health management in 2100. Advanced screening technologies, such as genomics and molecular diagnostics, will enable the identification of diseases at their earliest stages, when treatment options are most effective. Routine screenings for conditions such as cancer, cardiovascular diseases, and neurodegenerative disorders will become the norm, allowing for early intervention and improved patient outcomes.

To successfully implement population health management and preventive care, collaboration and coordination among various stakeholders will be essential. Healthcare providers, public health agencies, policymakers, and technology innovators must work together to create a supportive ecosystem that fosters a preventive mindset and facilitates the adoption of innovative technologies. It will require partnerships that transcend traditional health-care boundaries and leverage the power of interdisciplinary collaboration.

Furthermore, addressing health disparities and promoting health equity will be integral to population health management in 2100. Efforts must be made to ensure that preventive interventions and healthcare resources are accessible to all individuals, regardless of their socioeconomic status or geographic location. Bridging the gap in healthcare disparities will require targeted interventions, community engagement, and policies that address the underlying social determinants of health.

In conclusion, population health management and preventive care will shape the future of healthcare in 2100. Through the use of predictive analytics, AI algorithms, and big data, healthcare providers will identify high-risk populations and implement targeted interventions to prevent diseases and promote overall population health. Public health campaigns, lifestyle interventions, and early detection programs will be instrumental in creating a healthier future for all. Let us embrace this proactive approach to healthcare delivery, working together to build a world where prevention is the key to a healthier and more vibrant population.

6.Blockchain Technology and Secure Health Data Exchange:

The adoption of blockchain technology will ensure secure health data exchange and interoperability in 2100. Patient records, test results, and treatment histories will be stored in a decentralized and tamper-proof manner, enhancing data privacy and security. Blockchain-based platforms will enable seamless sharing of patient data between healthcare providers, facilitating comprehensive and coordinated care delivery. This technology will empower patients with control over their health data, enabling them to make informed decisions about their healthcare.

In the year 2100, the adoption of blockchain technology will revolutionize health data management, ensuring secure data exchange, interoperability, and patient empowerment.

At the heart of blockchain technology lies its decentralized and tamper-proof nature. In 2100, patient records, test results, and treatment histories will be securely stored on a blockchain network. This decentralized approach eliminates the need for a central authority to manage and authenticate health data. Instead, data will be distributed across a network of nodes, ensuring that no single entity has control over the entire dataset. This decentralization makes health data more resistant to unauthorized access, tampering, or data breaches.

With blockchain-based platforms, healthcare providers will be able to seamlessly share patient data, leading to comprehensive and coordinated care delivery. Imagine a scenario where a patient visits a specialist who needs access to their complete medical history. Instead of relying on fragmented records from different providers, the specialist can securely access the patient's comprehensive health record stored on the blockchain. This ensures that the specialist has all the necessary information to make informed decisions about the patient's care, leading to improved outcomes and reduced medical errors.

Furthermore, blockchain technology will empower patients with control over their health data. In 2100, patients will have the ability to manage their health records securely on the blockchain. They will be able to grant permission for healthcare providers to access their data, ensuring that only authorized individuals can view their sensitive information. This patient-centric approach gives individuals greater autonomy and allows them to actively participate in their healthcare decisions.

Blockchain also offers a solution to the interoperability challenges that have long plagued the healthcare industry. In 2100, blockchain-based systems will facilitate the seamless exchange of health data between different healthcare providers, regardless of their electronic health record (EHR) systems. By establishing standardized protocols and data formats, blockchain will enable interoperability and enhance data sharing, promoting better continuity of care and reducing the administrative burden on healthcare professionals.

Data privacy and security are of paramount importance in the era of digital health. Blockchain's cryptographic algorithms ensure that health data is encrypted and tamper-proof, protecting patient privacy and maintaining data integrity. Additionally, blockchain's distributed ledger technology ensures transparency, as any changes or access to health data are recorded and auditable. This transparency enhances trust between patients and healthcare providers, strengthening the overall healthcare ecosystem.

However, embracing blockchain technology in healthcare will require collaborative efforts and careful consideration of regulatory frameworks. Stakeholders, including healthcare providers, technology companies, policy-makers, and regulatory bodies, must work together to establish standards and guidelines for the adoption and implementation of blockchain. Ethical considerations and patient consent mechanisms should also be integrated into the design and implementation of blockchain-based health systems.

In conclusion, blockchain technology will revolutionize health data exchange and security in 2100. By leveraging its decentralized nature, blockchain ensures secure and tamper-proof storage of health data. Blockchain-based platforms will enable seamless sharing of patient data, promoting comprehensive and coordinated care delivery. Moreover, patients will have control over their health data, empowering them to make informed decisions about their healthcare. Let us embrace this transformative technology, working together to build a future where data privacy, security, and patient empowerment are at the forefront of healthcare.

7.Ethical Considerations and Human-Centered Care:

While technological advancements will drive healthcare delivery in 2100, ethical considerations and human-centered care must remain at the forefront. Balancing technological progress with patient autonomy, privacy, and the preservation of the patient-provider relationship will be essential. Robust ethical frameworks, guidelines, and regulations will guide the responsible and equitable use of technology in healthcare delivery, ensuring that the focus remains on improving patient outcomes and well-being.

As we look ahead to the year 2100, where technological advancements will reshape healthcare, it is crucial to strike a balance between progress and maintaining the fundamental principles of patient autonomy, privacy, and the preservation of the patient-provider relationship.

In this era of unprecedented innovation, technology will undoubtedly play a pivotal role in healthcare delivery. From AI-driven diagnostics to genomic medicine, robotics, and telemedicine, these advancements have the potential to revolutionize patient care and improve health outcomes. However, it is imperative that we approach these developments with a strong ethical foundation and a focus on human-centered care.

First and foremost, patient autonomy must remain paramount. As technology becomes more integrated into healthcare, patients must have the right to make informed decisions about their treatment options, the use of their health data, and the extent to which technology is involved in their care. Respecting patient autonomy means involving them in the decision-making process, providing them with comprehensive information, and ensuring that their choices are honored.

Privacy and confidentiality are also critical ethical considerations. In an era of digital health and interconnected systems, the protection of patient data becomes increasingly vital. Healthcare providers and technology developers must prioritize robust data security measures to safeguard patient privacy. Transparent policies and procedures should be in place to inform patients about how their data is collected, used, and stored. Additionally, patients should have control over their data and the ability to determine who has access to it.

Preserving the patient-provider relationship is another ethical imperative. While technology can enhance efficiency and improve healthcare outcomes, it must not replace the human touch and the empathetic connection between patients and healthcare providers. Even in a technologically advanced future, it is vital to maintain the role of healthcare professionals as compassionate caregivers who provide emotional support and personalized care. Technology should complement, rather than replace, the human element in healthcare.

To ensure responsible and equitable use of technology in healthcare delivery, robust ethical frameworks, guidelines, and regulations must be established. These frameworks should be developed collaboratively by healthcare professionals, policymakers, ethicists, and technology experts. They should address issues such as informed consent, transparency, data governance, algorithmic bias, and the equitable distribution of healthcare resources. Ongoing evaluation and adaptation of these frameworks will be necessary to keep pace with rapid technological advancements.

Furthermore, ethical considerations must extend beyond individual patient care to encompass broader societal impact. Healthcare disparities and equity must be addressed to ensure that advancements in technology do not further exacerbate existing inequalities. Efforts should be made to bridge the digital divide, promote access to healthcare resources, and eliminate biases in algorithms and data that could perpetuate disparities. Ethical decision-making should be guided by principles of justice, fairness, and inclusivity.

In conclusion, as we envision the future of healthcare in 2100, it is imperative that ethical considerations and human-centered care remain at the forefront. Technology will undoubtedly shape healthcare delivery, but we must ensure that patient autonomy, privacy, and the patient-provider relationship are upheld. Robust ethical frameworks and regulations will guide the responsible and equitable use of technology, with a focus on improving patient outcomes and well-being. By combining technological advancements with ethical principles, we can create a future where healthcare is compassionate, patient-centric, and inclusive.

The healthcare delivery landscape in 2100 will be marked by significant advancements, driven by technology, data, and patient-centered approaches. Telemedicine, AI-driven diagnostic systems, robotics, personalized medicine, and secure health data exchange will revolutionize access, efficiency, and the quality of care. However, ethical considerations, patient privacy, and the preservation of the human touch in healthcare must be carefully addressed. By leveraging advancements responsibly and ensuring equitable access, healthcare delivery in 2100 has the potential to

VI

Societal Paradigm Shifts

13

Global Governance and Diplomacy

The year 2100 presents a world that is intricately interconnected, with unprecedented technological advancements, complex global challenges, and evolving power dynamics. In this chapter, we explore the potential landscape of global governance and diplomacy in 2100, focusing on the frameworks, institutions, and diplomatic strategies that will shape international relations and address global issues.

1.Multi-Stakeholder Governance:

In 2100, global governance will likely shift towards a more inclusive and multi-stakeholder approach. Traditional nation-state-centered diplomacy will be complemented by the active participation of non-state actors, including civil society organizations, multinational corporations, and scientific communities. Decision-making processes will become more collaborative, seeking diverse perspectives and expertise to address complex challenges such as climate change, pandemics, and technological disruptions.

in the year 2100, where we can expect a significant shift towards a more inclusive and multi-stakeholder approach. In this future era, traditional nation-state-centered diplomacy will be complemented by active participation from a diverse range of non-state actors, including civil society organizations, multinational corporations, and scientific communities. This shift towards multi-stakeholder governance will enable more effective decision-making processes, as we tackle complex global challenges such as climate change,

133

pandemics, and technological disruptions.

In the year 2100, the interconnected nature of our world will demand a collaborative approach to governance. The traditional model of top-down decision-making by nation-states will no longer be sufficient to address the multifaceted challenges we face. Recognizing this, global governance structures will embrace the participation of diverse stakeholders to leverage their unique perspectives, expertise, and resources.

Non-state actors, such as civil society organizations, will play a crucial role in shaping global governance. These organizations, driven by their missions and values, bring grassroots perspectives and advocate for the interests of marginalized communities. Their participation in decision-making processes will ensure that governance addresses the needs and aspirations of the people they represent. By bridging the gap between citizens and decision-makers, civil society organizations will foster transparency, accountability, and inclusivity in global governance.

Multinational corporations will also have an active role to play in the governance of the future. As powerful global actors with immense resources and influence, these corporations will be expected to contribute to addressing societal challenges. With their expertise in innovation and technology, they can drive positive change and collaborate with governments and civil society to achieve shared goals. Ethical business practices, social responsibility, and sustainability will be essential principles guiding their participation in global governance.

Scientific communities will emerge as vital stakeholders in decision-making processes. Their expertise and evidence-based insights will inform policy development and response strategies for global challenges. Collaboration between scientists, policymakers, and other stakeholders will ensure that decisions are grounded in scientific knowledge and consider the long-term consequences of our actions. Through research, innovation, and evidence-based policymaking, scientific communities will contribute to the well-being of humanity and the planet.

In this multi-stakeholder governance model, decision-making processes will become more transparent, inclusive, and participatory. Dialogue platforms and collaborative mechanisms will be established to bring together diverse stakeholders, encouraging constructive discussions, and fostering mutual understanding. Embracing diverse perspectives will enable us to find comprehensive solutions to complex challenges that transcend national boundaries.

However, this shift towards multi-stakeholder governance also poses challenges. Balancing the interests and power dynamics among various stakeholders will require effective mechanisms for negotiation, cooperation, and conflict resolution. Robust frameworks and institutions will need to be in place to ensure accountability, protect the rights of individuals and communities, and prevent undue influence or capture by vested interests.

In conclusion, in the year 2100, we can anticipate a transformative shift towards multi-stakeholder governance in the global arena. This inclusive approach, which brings together nation-states, civil society organizations, multinational corporations, and scientific communities, will enable more effective decision-making processes to tackle complex global challenges. By embracing diverse perspectives, expertise, and resources, we can work collaboratively towards a more sustainable, equitable, and prosperous future for all. Let us strive for a governance model that truly represents the interests of humanity and fosters collective action for the betterment of our world.

2.Technology and Diplomatic Strategies:

Technological advancements will significantly impact global governance and diplomacy in 2100. Diplomatic strategies will incorporate emerging technologies, including artificial intelligence, blockchain, and advanced data analytics, to enhance decision-making, streamline processes, and strengthen global cooperation. Digital diplomacy, cyber diplomacy, and virtual diplomacy will play crucial roles in fostering international dialogue, promoting understanding, and resolving disputes in the digital era.

As we look ahead, it is evident that technological advancements will revolutionize diplomatic strategies and reshape the way nations interact on the global stage. Emerging technologies, such as artificial intelligence, blockchain, and advanced data analytics, will become integral tools in enhancing decision-making, streamlining processes, and strengthening global cooperation.

In the digital age, technology will enable new forms of diplomacy to thrive. Digital diplomacy, cyber diplomacy, and virtual diplomacy will play pivotal roles in fostering international dialogue, promoting understanding, and resolving disputes. These innovative approaches will leverage the power of technology to transcend geographical barriers and enhance communication among nations.

Artificial intelligence (AI) will be at the forefront of diplomatic strategies in 2100. AI algorithms will assist diplomats and decision-makers in analyzing vast amounts of data, identifying trends, and generating insights to inform policy and negotiation processes. AI-powered tools will help diplomats in forecasting scenarios, evaluating risks, and designing effective strategies. Additionally, AI can contribute to real-time translation and interpretation, facilitating smoother communication and understanding between different cultures and languages.

Blockchain technology will revolutionize diplomatic processes, particularly in ensuring trust, transparency, and security. The decentralized and tamper-proof nature of blockchain will enhance the integrity of diplomatic negotiations, agreements, and transactions. Blockchain-based platforms can provide secure and immutable records, enabling traceability and accountability in diplomatic exchanges. By leveraging blockchain, nations can build trust, streamline administrative procedures, and ensure the authenticity of digital documents and identities.

Advanced data analytics will empower diplomats with deeper insights into global trends, public sentiment, and social dynamics. By harnessing big data and sophisticated analytical tools, diplomats can gain a better understanding of the needs, aspirations, and concerns of diverse populations. Data-driven diplomacy will enable evidence-based decision-making, enhancing the effectiveness of diplomatic efforts and enabling more targeted interventions.

In the year 2100, digital diplomacy will transcend physical boundaries and foster virtual connections between nations. Virtual reality (VR) and augmented reality (AR) technologies will enable diplomats to engage in immersive virtual meetings, simulations, and negotiations. These technologies will create a sense of presence, facilitating meaningful interactions and strengthening diplomatic relations. Additionally, virtual diplomacy will enhance inclusivity by providing opportunities for participation and engagement to individuals and communities who may face geographical, financial, or physical constraints.

Cyber diplomacy will also be a critical aspect of diplomatic strategies in 2100. With the growing interconnectedness of the digital world, nations will need to cooperate and coordinate efforts to address cybersecurity challenges, combat cybercrime, and protect critical infrastructure. Cybersecurity diplomacy will involve the development of international norms, treaties, and agreements to govern responsible behavior in cyberspace. Diplomatic efforts will focus on building trust, sharing best practices, and developing frameworks for cooperation in addressing emerging cyber threats.

However, while technology brings immense opportunities, it also presents challenges. Ethical considerations, privacy concerns, and the potential for misuse must be carefully addressed. Diplomatic strategies must ensure that technology is used responsibly and in alignment with international laws and norms. Cooperation among nations will be crucial in establishing common standards, norms, and regulations to govern the use of technology in diplomacy.

In conclusion, in the year 2100, technology will play a transformative role in global governance and diplomacy. Artificial intelligence, blockchain, advanced data analytics, virtual diplomacy, and cyber diplomacy will shape diplomatic strategies and processes. Embracing these technologies will enhance decision-making, streamline communication, foster understanding, and strengthen global cooperation. By leveraging technology responsibly and collaboratively, we can build a future where nations work together more effectively, advancing peace, prosperity, and mutual understanding.

3.Climate Change and Sustainable Development:

By 2100, addressing climate change and promoting sustainable development will be paramount in global governance. International agreements, such as the Paris Agreement, will evolve and be reinforced with more ambitious targets and stricter enforcement mechanisms. Global institutions, such as the United Nations, will play a vital role in coordinating efforts, providing financial support, and facilitating technology transfer to ensure a sustainable and resilient future for all nations.

As we look ahead, it is evident that these issues will be at the forefront of global governance, demanding urgent and concerted action from nations around the world. International agreements, such as the Paris Agreement, will evolve, and global institutions like the United Nations will play a vital role in coordinating efforts to ensure a sustainable and resilient future for all.

In the year 2100, the consequences of climate change will become even more pronounced, impacting every aspect of our lives and the well-being of the planet. Rising temperatures, extreme weather events, sea-level rise, and biodiversity loss will continue to pose significant challenges. Recognizing the urgency of the situation, international agreements will undergo necessary transformations, reinforcing commitments and setting even more ambitious targets to limit global warming and mitigate the effects of climate change.

The Paris Agreement, which aims to keep global temperature rise well below 2 degrees Celsius above pre-industrial levels, will be a cornerstone of global climate action in 2100. Building upon its foundation, nations will work together to strengthen the agreement, implement robust mechanisms for accountability, and enhance transparency in reporting their progress. Stricter enforcement mechanisms will ensure that countries adhere to their commitments and take concrete actions to reduce greenhouse gas emissions.

Global institutions, particularly the United Nations, will play a crucial role in coordinating and facilitating international efforts to address climate change. They will provide a platform for collaboration, knowledge sharing, and capacity building among nations. Through platforms like the Conference of the Parties (COP) and the Intergovernmental Panel on Climate Change

(IPCC), scientific research and evidence will inform policy-making and guide international action. Financial support and technology transfer will be key components of global cooperation to assist developing nations in their transition to sustainable and low-carbon economies.

In the year 2100, sustainable development will be deeply integrated into global governance. Nations will strive to achieve the United Nations Sustainable Development Goals (SDGs), encompassing a broad range of issues, including poverty eradication, clean energy access, sustainable cities, responsible consumption and production, and conservation of biodiversity. Sustainable development will be at the core of national policies, with a focus on balancing economic growth, social well-being, and environmental protection.

Innovation and technology will be powerful drivers of sustainable development in 2100. Renewable energy sources, such as solar and wind power, will dominate the energy landscape, reducing reliance on fossil fuels. Advancements in clean technologies, energy storage, and efficient resource management will accelerate the transition to a low-carbon and circular economy. Sustainable agriculture practices, including precision farming and agroecology, will ensure food security while minimizing environmental impacts. Technology-driven solutions, such as smart cities and sustainable transport systems, will enhance the quality of life for urban populations while reducing carbon emissions.

However, addressing climate change and achieving sustainable development will require global cooperation, collective action, and a shift in mindset. It will demand the participation and commitment of governments, businesses, civil society, and individuals. Education, awareness, and behavior change will be crucial in fostering sustainable lifestyles and responsible consumption patterns.

In conclusion, in the year 2100, addressing climate change and promoting sustainable development will be paramount in global governance. International agreements, such as the Paris Agreement, will evolve and be reinforced with more ambitious targets and stricter enforcement mechanisms. Global institutions, particularly the United Nations, will play a vital role in coordinating efforts, providing financial support, and facilitating technology transfer. By working together, we can create a sustainable and resilient future, ensuring the well-being of present and future generations. Let us embrace the challenge and take decisive action for a better world.

4.Crisis Management and Global Security:

In 2100, global governance and diplomacy will face evolving security challenges, including cybersecurity threats, geopolitical conflicts, and regional instabilities. Strengthened international cooperation, early warning systems, and crisis response mechanisms will be essential to manage and mitigate such crises. Regional organizations and alliances will collaborate closely with global institutions to maintain peace, prevent conflicts, and address security threats collectively.

As we look ahead, it is evident that global governance and diplomacy will confront evolving security challenges that demand swift and coordinated action. Cybersecurity threats, geopolitical conflicts, and regional instabilities will pose significant risks to global peace and stability. To effectively manage and mitigate these crises, strengthened international cooperation, early warning systems, and crisis response mechanisms will be essential.

In the digital age, cybersecurity threats will be a major concern for nations worldwide. Rapid technological advancements and increased interconnectedness will expose governments, businesses, and individuals to cyber attacks and data breaches. In response, global governance structures will prioritize cybersecurity measures, fostering international cooperation to develop norms, protocols, and mechanisms for information sharing and joint response to cyber threats. Collaboration between governments, private sector entities, and civil society will be crucial in enhancing cyber resilience, safeguarding critical infrastructure, and protecting the privacy and security of individuals.

Geopolitical conflicts and regional instabilities will continue to be significant challenges in 2100. Disputes over resources, territorial claims, and ideological differences may give rise to tensions and conflicts among nations. In this context, global governance will rely on strong diplomatic efforts to prevent conflicts, promote dialogue, and facilitate peaceful resolutions. Regional organizations and alliances will play a crucial role in maintaining stability and fostering cooperation among neighboring countries. Robust conflict prevention mechanisms, early warning systems, and effective mediation will be employed to mitigate potential conflicts and ensure peaceful resolutions.

Crisis response mechanisms will undergo significant advancements in the year 2100. Early warning systems, leveraging advanced technologies and data analytics, will enable the timely detection of emerging crises, allowing for proactive and preventive interventions. Global institutions, such as the United Nations and regional organizations, will strengthen their capabilities to coordinate and respond to crises effectively. Rapid deployment of humanitarian aid, peacekeeping forces, and crisis management experts will be crucial in providing immediate support and stability to affected regions.

International cooperation will be the bedrock of crisis management and global security in 2100. Global governance structures, including the United Nations Security Council, will play a pivotal role in facilitating dialogue, negotiation, and consensus-building among nations. Collaboration between developed and developing countries will be essential to address security challenges in an equitable and inclusive manner. Capacity building, technical assistance, and financial support will be provided to countries facing security threats, enabling them to enhance their resilience and contribute to global stability.

Furthermore, the integration of advanced technologies, such as artificial intelligence, satellite imaging, and remote sensing, will significantly enhance crisis management capabilities. These technologies will provide real-time information, situational awareness, and predictive analysis, enabling more effective decision-making and response strategies. Moreover, innovative communication tools and platforms will facilitate rapid information sharing and coordination among international actors during crises, ensuring a cohesive and synchronized response.

In conclusion, in the year 2100, crisis management and global security will be paramount in global governance and diplomacy. Strengthened international cooperation, early warning systems, and crisis response mechanisms will be essential to manage and mitigate evolving security challenges. Regional organizations and alliances will collaborate closely with global institutions to maintain peace, prevent conflicts, and address security threats collectively. By working together, nations can create a safer and more secure world for future generations. Let us embrace the challenges ahead and strive for a future of peace and stability.

5.Human Rights and Social Justice:

The promotion and protection of human rights and social justice will remain central to global governance in 2100. International norms and standards will continue to evolve, ensuring the rights and well-being of individuals across borders. Gender equality, racial justice, and inclusivity will be prioritized, with global institutions and diplomatic efforts working towards creating a more equitable and just world.

As we envision the future, it is evident that the promotion and protection of human rights will remain central to our collective efforts. International norms and standards will continue to evolve, ensuring the rights and well-being of individuals across borders. In the pursuit of a more equitable and just world, gender equality, racial justice, and inclusivity will be prioritized, with global institutions and diplomatic efforts playing a crucial role.

In the year 2100, the recognition and protection of human rights will be firmly ingrained in the fabric of global governance. The Universal Declaration of Human Rights, adopted in 1948, will continue to serve as a foundational document guiding the principles of human rights. However, our understanding of human rights will continue to evolve, addressing emerging challenges and advancing the rights of marginalized and vulnerable populations.

Gender equality will be a fundamental principle of global governance in 2100. Efforts to eradicate gender discrimination, empower women, and promote gender diversity will be at the forefront of diplomatic agendas. Gender-based violence, unequal access to education and healthcare, and discriminatory practices will be vigorously addressed. Policies and initiatives will be implemented to ensure equal opportunities, representation, and participation for women in all spheres of life. By promoting gender equality, we will create a more just and prosperous world for everyone.

Racial justice will also be a key focus in the year 2100. Recognizing the deep-rooted impacts of historical injustices and systemic discrimination, global governance will prioritize the eradication of racial discrimination and the promotion of racial equality. Efforts to address racial disparities in education, employment, criminal justice, and healthcare will be undertaken, with a commitment to dismantling structures that perpetuate inequality. Embracing diversity and inclusivity will be seen as essential for social progress, fostering a world where every individual is valued and respected regardless of their race or ethnicity.

Inclusivity will be a guiding principle of global governance in 2100. Efforts will be made to ensure the participation and representation of all individuals, including marginalized groups, in decision-making processes at all levels. People with disabilities, indigenous communities, LGBTQ+ individuals, and other marginalized populations will have their voices heard, their rights protected, and their perspectives integrated into policies and programs. By embracing inclusivity, we will foster a society that values diversity and recognizes the inherent dignity and worth of every individual.

Global institutions, such as the United Nations and regional organizations, will play a vital role in advancing human rights and social justice. They will serve as platforms for dialogue, collaboration, and consensus-building among nations. Through diplomatic efforts, international norms and standards will be strengthened, promoting human rights principles and holding governments accountable for their commitments. Monitoring mechanisms, reporting systems, and independent human rights commissions will ensure transparency and accountability in upholding human rights obligations.

Moreover, technology will play a transformative role in advancing human rights and social justice in 2100. Digital platforms and social media will amplify the voices of marginalized communities, exposing human rights abuses and fostering global solidarity. Technological advancements, such as blockchain and artificial intelligence, will enhance transparency, accountability, and data privacy, ensuring the protection of human rights in an increasingly interconnected world.

In conclusion, in the year 2100, the promotion and protection of human rights and social justice will remain central to global governance. Efforts will be made to advance gender equality, racial justice, and inclusivity, recognizing the inherent dignity and worth of every individual. Global institutions and diplomatic efforts will drive progress, ensuring the evolution of international norms and standards to meet emerging challenges. Let us commit ourselves to this noble cause, working together to create a world where human rights are universally respected, and social justice prevails.

6.Ethical Considerations and Cultural Sensitivity:

In 2100, global governance and diplomacy will grapple with ethical considerations and cultural sensitivity. As societies become more interconnected, respecting diverse cultural values, religious beliefs, and ethical frameworks will be crucial. Diplomatic efforts will prioritize dialogue, understanding, and mutual respect, ensuring that policies and decisions respect the rights and aspirations of all nations and communities.

As our world becomes increasingly interconnected, it is imperative that we recognize and respect diverse cultural values, religious beliefs, and ethical frameworks. In the pursuit of a harmonious global community, diplomatic efforts will prioritize dialogue, understanding, and mutual respect, ensuring that policies and decisions respect the rights and aspirations of all nations and communities.

In the year 2100, ethical considerations will be at the forefront of global governance. As technological advancements continue to reshape our societies, it is essential that we carefully navigate the ethical implications of these innovations. We must weigh the potential benefits against potential harms and ensure that emerging technologies are developed and deployed in a manner that upholds human rights, privacy, and dignity. Ethical frameworks and guidelines will guide the responsible and equitable use of technologies such as artificial intelligence, genetic engineering, and robotics, ensuring that they are harnessed for the collective good while avoiding unintended consequences.

Cultural sensitivity will also play a central role in global governance and diplomacy in 2100. As our world becomes more interconnected, it is essential to recognize and respect the diversity of cultural values, traditions, and practices that exist among nations and communities. Diplomatic efforts will prioritize dialogue and mutual understanding, fostering an environment where different cultures can coexist and thrive. Recognizing and celebrating cultural diversity will not only strengthen diplomatic relations but also contribute to a more peaceful and harmonious world.

Moreover, global governance structures will strive to incorporate cultural sensitivity into policy-making processes. By involving diverse perspectives and engaging in meaningful consultation with affected communities, policymakers can ensure that decisions take into account the cultural context and the specific needs and aspirations of different societies. This approach will promote inclusivity, empowerment, and ownership, fostering a sense of shared responsibility in shaping our collective future.

In the year 2100, diplomatic efforts will aim to bridge cultural divides and build trust among nations. Cultural diplomacy will play a pivotal role in fostering understanding, respect, and cooperation. Cultural exchanges, educational programs, and collaborative initiatives will be encouraged to promote intercultural dialogue and build lasting connections between societies. By engaging in open and respectful conversations, we can learn from one another, challenge stereotypes, and foster a global community that appreciates the richness and diversity of human cultures.

Furthermore, global governance and diplomacy will prioritize the protection and promotion of cultural heritage. Preserving cultural artifacts, languages, and traditional practices will be seen as essential for maintaining cultural diversity and fostering intergenerational continuity. Efforts to safeguard cultural heritage from destruction, theft, and appropriation will be undertaken, ensuring that future generations can draw inspiration from their rich cultural heritage.

In conclusion, in the year 2100, global governance and diplomacy will grapple with ethical considerations and cultural sensitivity. Respecting diverse cultural values, religious beliefs, and ethical frameworks will be crucial in fostering a harmonious global community. Diplomatic efforts will prioritize dialogue, understanding, and mutual respect, ensuring that policies and decisions respect the rights and aspirations of all nations and communities. By embracing ethical considerations and cultural sensitivity, we can foster a world where diversity is celebrated, and the collective well-being of humanity is upheld. Let us work together to build a future where cultural richness and ethical principles guide our global interactions.

7.Global Health Governance:

The lessons learned from the COVID-19 pandemic will shape global health governance in 2100. Strengthened international collaboration, early detection systems, and coordinated response mechanisms will be in place to effectively address future pandemics. Global health institutions will work closely with national governments, civil society organizations, and the private sector to ensure access to affordable and equitable healthcare for all.

I would like to discuss the critical topic of global health governance in the year 2100. The lessons we have learned from the COVID-19 pandemic have underscored the need for robust and collaborative global health systems. As we look ahead, it is evident that strengthened international collaboration, early detection systems, and coordinated response mechanisms will be key to effectively addressing future pandemics and promoting the well-being of all individuals.

The COVID-19 pandemic has been a stark reminder of the interconnectedness of our world and the importance of global cooperation in matters of public health. In 2100, global health governance will be characterized by enhanced international collaboration and coordination. Global health institutions, such as the World Health Organization (WHO), will work closely with national governments, civil society organizations, and the private sector to establish frameworks that facilitate timely information sharing, joint research efforts, and the equitable distribution of healthcare resources.

One of the lessons learned from the COVID-19 pandemic is the need for early detection systems. In 2100, global health governance will prioritize the development and implementation of robust surveillance and monitoring mechanisms to detect the emergence of new diseases and pandemics at the earliest possible stages. These systems will rely on advanced technologies, such as artificial intelligence and big data analytics, to analyze vast amounts of health data and identify potential health threats in real-time. By detecting and responding to outbreaks swiftly, we can minimize their impact and prevent them from escalating into global crises.

Coordinated response mechanisms will also be a cornerstone of global health governance in 2100. The COVID-19 pandemic has demonstrated the importance of a unified and coordinated global response to address public health emergencies. In the future, global health institutions will work closely with national governments to develop comprehensive preparedness plans, strengthen healthcare systems, and establish mechanisms for rapid deployment of medical personnel, supplies, and treatments to affected regions. Collaborative efforts in research and development will be prioritized to accelerate the discovery of vaccines, therapeutics, and diagnostics for emerging diseases.

Equitable access to healthcare will be a core principle of global health governance in 2100. The COVID-19 pandemic has highlighted the existing health disparities and inequities that exist around the world. In the future, global health institutions will work tirelessly to ensure that access to affordable and quality healthcare is a fundamental right for all individuals, regardless of their socio-economic status or geographic location. Efforts will be made to strengthen healthcare systems in underserved regions, improve health infrastructure, and enhance healthcare workforce capacity. Additionally, initiatives to promote affordable and equitable access to essential medicines and vaccines will be pursued to protect the most vulnerable populations.

In conclusion, the lessons learned from the COVID-19 pandemic will shape global health governance in 2100. Strengthened international collaboration, early detection systems, and coordinated response mechanisms will be in place to effectively address future pandemics and ensure the well-being of all individuals. Global health institutions, in collaboration with national governments, civil society organizations, and the private sector, will work tirelessly to ensure equitable access to affordable healthcare for everyone. By investing in robust global health governance, we can build a future where the health and well-being of all individuals are safeguarded.

In 2100, global governance and diplomacy will navigate an increasingly complex and interconnected world. Multi-stakeholder governance, technological integration, sustainable development, crisis management, human rights, and cultural sensitivity will be integral to international relations. By fostering inclusive and collaborative approaches, global institutions and diplomatic efforts can effectively address the pressing global challenges of the future, promoting peace, security, and sustainable development for the benefit of all nations and humanity as a whole.

14

Cultural Blending and Identity in a Connected World

The year 2100 presents a world characterized by unprecedented connectivity, cultural exchange, and technological advancements. As societies become increasingly interconnected, the blending of cultures and the evolution of identities will shape the global landscape. This chapter explores the dynamics of cultural blending and the transformation of identity in a connected world in 2100, examining the opportunities, challenges, and implications for individuals and societies.

1.Globalization and Cultural Exchange:

In 2100, globalization will continue to facilitate cultural exchange on an unprecedented scale. Advances in transportation, communication, and digital technologies will enable instantaneous connections and interactions across borders. This continuous exchange of ideas, values, and traditions will contribute to a rich tapestry of cultural blending, fostering cross-cultural understanding and appreciation.

As we look ahead, it is evident that globalization will continue to facilitate an unprecedented level of intercultural connectivity and interaction. Advances in transportation, communication, and digital technologies will transform the way we connect and engage with people from diverse backgrounds, leading to a rich tapestry of cultural blending that fosters cross-cultural understanding and appreciation.

In 2100, the world will be more interconnected than ever before. The boundaries that once separated nations and cultures will become more fluid, allowing for the free flow of ideas, values, and traditions. This interconnectedness will be facilitated by advancements in transportation, enabling individuals to travel effortlessly across the globe. Whether it's for business, education, or leisure, people will have the opportunity to immerse themselves in different cultures, learn from one another, and embrace new perspectives.

Communication technologies will also play a vital role in shaping cultural exchange in 2100. The advent of high-speed internet, social media platforms, and virtual reality will enable instantaneous connections and interactions across borders. People will be able to engage in real-time conversations, share experiences, and collaborate with individuals from different cultural backgrounds. This level of connectivity will break down barriers and foster a sense of global community, where cultural exchange becomes a natural and celebrated part of everyday life.

Digital technologies will further enhance cultural exchange by providing access to a vast array of cultural resources and experiences. Online platforms will offer opportunities to explore different languages, cuisines, music, art, and literature from around the world. Virtual reality experiences will allow individuals to step into the shoes of someone from a different culture, immersing themselves in their customs, traditions, and daily lives. These technological advancements will not only promote cultural understanding but also enable individuals to develop a deep appreciation for the diversity of our global society.

The continuous exchange of ideas, values, and traditions will have profound implications for cross-cultural understanding and appreciation. Cultural blending will lead to the emergence of new hybrid cultures that reflect the influences and contributions of various societies. This blending will not erase or diminish individual cultural identities but rather create a mosaic of diversity where different cultural expressions coexist and enrich one another.

In this interconnected world, cultural exchange will play a crucial role in breaking down stereotypes, challenging prejudices, and promoting peace and harmony. By engaging in open and respectful dialogue, we can learn from one another, build bridges of understanding, and appreciate the richness and uniqueness of different cultural perspectives. This cultural exchange will foster a global community that values inclusivity, empathy, and respect for all individuals, regardless of their cultural backgrounds.

As we embrace the opportunities and challenges of globalization in 2100, it is essential to approach cultural exchange with a sense of openness and curiosity. We must recognize that cultural diversity is a strength to be celebrated and that mutual respect and understanding are vital for peaceful coexistence in our interconnected world. By embracing cultural exchange, we can build bridges of understanding that transcend borders, foster cross-cultural collaborations, and create a brighter and more inclusive future for all.

In conclusion, in 2100, globalization will continue to facilitate cultural exchange on an unprecedented scale. Advances in transportation, communication, and digital technologies will enable instantaneous connections and interactions across borders. This continuous exchange of ideas, values, and traditions will contribute to a rich tapestry of cultural blending, fostering cross-cultural understanding and appreciation. Let us embrace this interconnectedness and strive to build a global community that celebrates diversity, promotes inclusivity, and values the power of cultural exchange.

2.Hybrid Identities and Cosmopolitanism:

As cultures blend, individuals will develop hybrid identities, combining elements from multiple cultural backgrounds. This hybridity will give rise to a sense of cosmopolitanism, where individuals identify with a global community while maintaining connections to their local cultures. This cosmopolitan outlook will foster inclusivity, empathy, and a broader understanding of the diverse perspectives that shape our interconnected world.

As globalization continues to shape our world, cultural blending will give rise to individuals with hybrid identities, who draw from multiple cultural backgrounds and experiences. This blending of cultures will foster a sense of cosmopolitanism, where individuals identify with a global community while maintaining a deep connection to their local cultures.

In 2100, the world will be a tapestry of diverse cultural expressions and influences. As people from different cultural backgrounds interact and share experiences, their identities will naturally evolve and reflect this cultural blending. Individuals will embrace the richness of their heritage while also incorporating elements from other cultures, creating unique and multifaceted identities that transcend traditional boundaries.

Hybrid identities represent a departure from the notion of a singular, fixed cultural identity. Instead, individuals will find themselves at the intersection of different cultural traditions, languages, and beliefs. They will navigate the complexities of their hybrid identities, weaving together different cultural threads to create a tapestry that is uniquely their own.

The emergence of hybrid identities will contribute to the development of a cosmopolitan outlook—a sense of belonging to a global community. Individuals with hybrid identities will recognize that their experiences are not limited to a single cultural framework but are shaped by interactions with people from diverse backgrounds. This cosmopolitan perspective encourages empathy, inclusivity, and a broader understanding of the diverse perspectives that shape our interconnected world.

Cosmopolitanism fosters an appreciation for the interdependence of cultures and promotes cross-cultural dialogue and collaboration. It encourages individuals to embrace cultural differences, challenge preconceived notions, and seek common ground. By recognizing the value of diverse perspectives, cosmopolitan individuals contribute to a more inclusive and harmonious global society.

The embrace of hybrid identities and cosmopolitanism in 2100 will have far-reaching implications. It will challenge traditional notions of national and cultural boundaries, as individuals forge connections that transcend geopolitical borders. This interconnectedness will promote cultural exchange, collaboration, and the sharing of knowledge and ideas, ultimately leading to innovation and progress.

However, it is important to note that the emergence of hybrid identities and cosmopolitanism should not erase or diminish the significance of individual cultural traditions. Instead, it should encourage the celebration and preservation of cultural heritage while fostering an open-mindedness that embraces the diversity of human experiences.

In conclusion, in 2100, the blending of cultures will give rise to individuals with hybrid identities, who draw from multiple cultural backgrounds and experiences. This blending will foster a sense of cosmopolitanism—a recognition of a global community and a deep connection to local cultures. The embrace of hybrid identities and cosmopolitanism will promote inclusivity, empathy, and a broader understanding of the diverse perspectives that shape our interconnected world. Let us celebrate the beauty of cultural blending and strive for a future where our shared humanity transcends borders and unites us all.

3.Technological Influences on Identity:

Technology will play a significant role in shaping identities in 2100. The proliferation of social media, virtual reality, and augmented reality will offer individuals new platforms for self-expression and identity exploration. Online communities and digital spaces will provide opportunities for individuals to connect with like-minded individuals globally, forming virtual identities that transcend geographical boundaries.

As we continue to witness advancements in social media, virtual reality, and augmented reality, technology will increasingly shape how individuals perceive and express their identities. In this digital age, online platforms and digital spaces will provide unprecedented opportunities for self-expression and identity exploration.

In 2100, technology will break down geographical barriers, allowing individuals to connect with like-minded individuals from all corners of the globe. Online communities will provide spaces where people can come together based on shared interests, passions, and values, creating virtual identities that transcend traditional notions of identity defined by geographic boundaries. These digital communities will offer a sense of belonging and allow individuals to find acceptance and support from others who understand their unique experiences and perspectives.

Social media will continue to evolve and exert a significant influence on identity formation. Individuals will have the ability to curate and present different aspects of their lives, carefully selecting what they choose to share with the world. This curated online presence can shape perceptions of identity and influence how individuals are perceived by others. It is important to recognize that the digital persona individuals create may not fully represent their complex and multidimensional identities.

Virtual reality and augmented reality technologies will further revolutionize identity exploration. They will allow individuals to step into virtual worlds, assuming different roles and experimenting with different aspects of their identities. This immersive experience will offer a safe space for individuals to explore and understand themselves better. Virtual reality can enable individuals to experience life from different perspectives, promoting empathy and fostering a deeper understanding of diverse identities.

While technology opens up exciting possibilities for self-expression and identity exploration, it is crucial to navigate this landscape with caution. The influence of technology on identity should be viewed critically, recognizing both its potential benefits and risks. As individuals engage with online platforms and virtual communities, it is essential to maintain a sense of authenticity and integrity, embracing the complexities of their identities and respecting the identities of others.

Moreover, it is important to strike a balance between the digital world and the physical world. While technology can enhance our connections and experiences, it should not replace real-life interactions and human connections. Building meaningful relationships and engaging in face-to-face interactions will remain fundamental to the development of a well-rounded and authentic identity.

In conclusion, technology will have a profound impact on identity in 2100. Online platforms, virtual reality, and augmented reality will offer individuals new avenues for self-expression and identity exploration. The ability to connect with like-minded individuals globally will shape virtual identities that transcend geographical boundaries. However, it is essential to approach technology with mindfulness and authenticity, recognizing the complexities of identity and embracing the diversity of human experiences. Let us leverage technology to foster understanding, empathy, and respect for the multifaceted identities that define us as individuals and as a global community.

4.Challenges of Cultural Blending:

While cultural blending brings about numerous benefits, it also presents challenges in maintaining cultural diversity and preserving unique traditions. The risk of cultural homogenization and the erosion of local customs and languages will require careful attention. In 2100, efforts to safeguard cultural heritage and promote cultural diversity will be vital to ensure the richness and variety of human expression.

While cultural blending undoubtedly brings about numerous benefits, it also presents us with the responsibility of preserving cultural diversity and safeguarding unique traditions. As our world becomes increasingly interconnected, the risk of cultural homogenization and the erosion of local customs and languages becomes a pressing concern.

Cultural blending occurs as a result of globalization, migration, technological advancements, and the ease of travel. It offers us the opportunity to exchange ideas, beliefs, and practices, fostering cross-cultural understanding and enriching our collective human experience. Through cultural blending, we gain exposure to new perspectives, art forms, and ways of life, leading to a more inclusive and interconnected world.

However, amidst this blending of cultures, there is a risk of cultural assimilation, where dominant cultures overshadow and absorb smaller, marginalized cultures. This process can result in the loss of unique traditions, languages, and ways of life that have been passed down through generations. It is crucial to recognize the value of cultural diversity and take proactive measures to preserve and celebrate the rich tapestry of human expression.

In 2100, one of the significant challenges we will face is striking a balance between cultural blending and the preservation of cultural heritage. It will require careful attention and deliberate efforts to ensure that no culture is marginalized or erased in the process. Preserving and revitalizing endangered languages, promoting traditional arts and crafts, and safeguarding intangible cultural heritage will be essential components of this endeavor.

Education plays a vital role in addressing these challenges. By fostering cultural literacy and promoting intercultural dialogue, we can cultivate an appreciation for diverse cultures and encourage individuals to value and respect their own heritage and the heritage of others. Schools and educational institutions should integrate multicultural education into their curricula, providing students with opportunities to learn about different cultures, traditions, and perspectives.

Furthermore, efforts should be made to empower local communities to preserve and transmit their cultural heritage. This can be achieved through community-led initiatives, cultural festivals, and the establishment of cultural preservation centers. Supporting and amplifying the voices of indigenous communities and marginalized groups will be crucial in ensuring that their cultural practices are recognized and valued.

Technological advancements, while contributing to cultural blending, can also be harnessed to preserve and promote cultural diversity. Digital platforms can serve as repositories for cultural artifacts, traditional music, stories, and languages, making them accessible to a global audience. Online communities can be created to connect individuals who share a common heritage and provide a space for cultural exchange and preservation.

In conclusion, while cultural blending brings about numerous benefits, it is essential to address the challenges it poses. Preserving cultural diversity and safeguarding unique traditions require deliberate efforts and a commitment to celebrating the richness and variety of human expression. By promoting cultural literacy, supporting local communities, and leveraging technology, we can create a world where cultural blending coexists with the preservation of cultural heritage. Let us embrace our shared humanity while valuing the diversity that makes us unique.

5.Identity Politics and Conflict:

The blending of cultures can also lead to identity politics and potential conflicts. In a connected world, clashes between different cultural, religious, and ethnic groups may arise. It will be essential to foster inclusive dialogues, promote mutual understanding, and respect diverse identities to mitigate tensions and build harmonious coexistence.

As our world becomes increasingly connected, the collision of different cultural, religious, and ethnic identities can create challenges that need to be addressed with wisdom and empathy.

Identity politics refers to the mobilization of political and social movements based on the shared identities of individuals. These identities can stem from factors such as race, ethnicity, religion, gender, or sexual orientation. While the recognition and celebration of diverse identities are important aspects of social progress, it is crucial to navigate the complexities that arise from these identities coming into contact with one another.

In a connected world, where cultures interact and influence one another, clashes between different identity groups can occur. Conflicts may arise due to differences in beliefs, values, and perspectives, as well as power imbalances and historical grievances. These conflicts can manifest at various levels, from individual interactions to larger societal tensions.

To address these challenges, fostering inclusive dialogues is paramount. Open and respectful communication is essential for promoting mutual understanding and finding common ground. It requires actively listening to different perspectives, acknowledging the experiences of others, and seeking to bridge divides rather than deepen them. It is through dialogue that we can challenge stereotypes, debunk misconceptions, and foster empathy between different identity groups.

Furthermore, promoting mutual understanding goes hand in hand with cultivating cultural literacy and education. By teaching about the histories, traditions, and contributions of diverse cultures, we can foster appreciation and respect for the identities of others. Education should emphasize the value of diversity and the importance of embracing multiple identities without undermining the rights and dignity of any group.

In addition, it is crucial to create spaces that encourage the exploration and celebration of identities while promoting peaceful coexistence. Communities, institutions, and governments should work together to foster inclusive environments where all individuals feel valued, respected, and able to express their identities freely. This can be achieved through policies that promote equal rights, non-discrimination, and social justice.

Conflict resolution mechanisms should also be in place to address tensions that may arise between identity groups. Mediation, reconciliation, and restorative justice approaches can facilitate the resolution of conflicts and promote healing. It is important to promote dialogue and understanding not only at the individual level but also within communities, institutions, and nations.

Ultimately, the goal is to build a society that respects and embraces diversity while promoting harmonious coexistence. This requires a collective effort to challenge divisive ideologies, promote empathy, and foster a sense of shared humanity. By recognizing the interconnectedness of our identities and seeking to understand and appreciate the identities of others, we can build bridges of understanding and work towards a more inclusive and peaceful world.

In conclusion, while the blending of cultures can lead to identity politics and potential conflicts, it is crucial that we approach these challenges with openness, empathy, and a commitment to dialogue. By fostering inclusive conversations, promoting mutual understanding, and valuing the diversity of identities, we can navigate the complexities of a connected world and build a future characterized by peace, respect, and unity.

6.Education and Intercultural Competence:

Education systems in 2100 will adapt to the interconnected world, emphasizing intercultural competence and global citizenship. Curricula will focus on promoting cultural awareness, empathy, and effective communication across cultures. Educational institutions will play a critical role in nurturing open-mindedness and equipping individuals with the skills to navigate and appreciate the complexities of cultural blending.

As our global society becomes increasingly interconnected, it is essential to prepare the next generation to navigate and appreciate the complexities of diverse cultures.

In the year 2100, education systems will adapt to meet the demands of a rapidly changing world. Curricula will go beyond traditional subjects and prioritize the development of intercultural competence and global citizenship. Students will be exposed to a wide range of cultural perspectives, histories, and traditions, fostering cultural awareness and appreciation from an early age.

One of the key goals of education in 2100 will be to promote empathy and effective communication across cultures. Students will learn to recognize and challenge their own biases and assumptions, developing the ability to see the world through different lenses. They will be encouraged to engage in respectful dialogue, actively listen to diverse perspectives, and seek common ground.

Educational institutions will serve as catalysts for cultural exchange and understanding. Collaborative projects and exchange programs will bring students from different cultural backgrounds together, creating opportunities for meaningful interactions and the sharing of experiences. By working on shared goals and projects, students will learn to appreciate the value of diversity and develop the skills needed to collaborate across cultures.

Furthermore, technology will play a vital role in enhancing intercultural education. Virtual reality and augmented reality technologies will provide immersive experiences, allowing students to virtually visit different countries, explore cultural landmarks, and interact with individuals from diverse backgrounds. This integration of technology will provide students with a deeper understanding of the world and promote a sense of global interconnectedness.

In addition to fostering intercultural competence, education in 2100 will emphasize the importance of global citizenship. Students will learn about global challenges such as climate change, poverty, and inequality, and explore ways to address these issues collectively. They will be encouraged to think critically, develop solutions, and actively engage in making a positive impact on a global scale.

To support the development of intercultural competence, teachers themselves will receive specialized training. They will be equipped with the knowledge and skills to facilitate meaningful discussions, challenge stereotypes, and create inclusive learning environments. Professional development programs will enable educators to stay up-to-date with the latest research and best practices in intercultural education.

By emphasizing intercultural competence in education, we can foster a generation of individuals who are prepared to thrive in a diverse and interconnected world. They will possess the skills to navigate cultural differences, resolve conflicts peacefully, and contribute to a more inclusive and harmonious global society.

In conclusion, education in 2100 will play a pivotal role in promoting intercultural competence and global citizenship. Through a curriculum that emphasizes cultural awareness, empathy, and effective communication, students will develop the skills needed to navigate the complexities of cultural blending. By fostering a sense of global interconnectedness and nurturing open-mindedness, we can build a future where diversity is celebrated, understanding is cultivated, and collaboration across cultures is the norm.

7.Cultural Preservation and Innovation:

In 2100, striking a balance between cultural preservation and innovation will be crucial. While cultural blending fosters new ideas and artistic expressions, it is essential to preserve traditional practices, languages, and indigenous knowledge. Efforts to safeguard cultural heritage and provide opportunities for cultural expression will contribute to the richness and diversity of global culture.

In a connected world in 2100, cultural blending and evolving identities will be defining features of human experience. Embracing cultural diversity, fostering inclusivity, and promoting intercultural dialogue will be essential for the peaceful coexistence of individuals and societies. By navigating the challenges and opportunities of cultural blending, we can cultivate a global community that celebrates its diverse heritage while fostering a shared sense of interconnectedness and collective responsibility.

VII

Ethical Dilemmas and Moral Choices

15

Artificial Intelligence and Ethics

As artificial intelligence (AI) continues to advance rapidly, the ethical considerations surrounding its development and use become increasingly significant. In the year 2100, AI systems will have reached unprecedented levels of sophistication, prompting profound questions about the ethical implications and societal impact of AI. This chapter explores the intersection of AI and ethics in 2100, examining the challenges, dilemmas, and potential solutions that arise as AI becomes deeply integrated into various aspects of human life.

1.Ethical Frameworks for AI:

In 2100, the development and deployment of AI will require robust ethical frameworks to guide its application. These frameworks will encompass principles such as transparency, accountability, fairness, and human well-being. Ethical guidelines will govern AI's decision-making capabilities, data usage, privacy protection, and potential consequences. International collaborations and agreements will aim to establish global standards to ensure the responsible and ethical use of AI technologies.

Fairness will be another critical ethical consideration for AI. Efforts will be made to ensure that AI systems do not perpetuate or amplify existing societal biases. Ethical frameworks will guide the development of AI algorithms that are sensitive to diversity, inclusivity, and equal treatment. The aim will be to eliminate discriminatory practices and ensure equitable access and outcomes for all individuals, regardless of their background.

Moreover, human well-being will be at the core of AI ethics. The goal will be to design AI systems that enhance human capabilities, improve quality of life, and promote societal progress. AI will be employed to tackle complex global challenges, such as healthcare, climate change, and poverty, with the aim of benefiting humanity as a whole. The ethical frameworks will emphasize the importance of prioritizing human values, dignity, and safety in the development and deployment of AI technologies.

To establish a global consensus on AI ethics, international collaborations and agreements will be essential. Countries, organizations, and stakeholders will work together to develop and implement ethical standards and guidelines that transcend borders. These global standards will serve as a reference point, ensuring the responsible and ethical use of AI technologies and preventing the misuse or abuse of AI for malicious purposes.

Furthermore, ongoing dialogue and engagement with diverse perspectives will be crucial in shaping and evolving AI ethics. Public input, interdisciplinary collaboration, and stakeholder engagement will help address the ethical complexities of AI, considering diverse cultural, social, and ethical contexts. This participatory approach will ensure that the development and deployment of AI technologies align with societal values and aspirations.

In conclusion, in 2100, robust ethical frameworks will guide the development and deployment of AI technologies. These frameworks will encompass principles of transparency, accountability, fairness, and human well-being. Through international collaborations and agreements, global standards for AI ethics will be established to ensure the responsible and ethical use of AI technologies. By prioritizing ethical considerations, we can harness the power of AI to benefit humanity, while upholding our values and safeguarding our collective well-being.

2. AI and Human Autonomy:

As AI systems become more sophisticated, questions surrounding human autonomy and agency will arise. In 2100, it will be crucial to strike a balance between AI's ability to assist and augment human decision-making while respecting individual autonomy. Ethical considerations will revolve around issues such as AI's impact on personal choices, privacy, and the potential for undue influence. Safeguards and regulations will be implemented to protect human agency and ensure that AI is designed to empower individuals rather than control them.

As AI systems become increasingly sophisticated and integrated into our lives, questions will arise regarding the impact of AI on human autonomy and agency. It is essential that we navigate this relationship carefully, ensuring that AI technologies respect and enhance human autonomy while avoiding undue influence or control.

In 2100, AI systems will possess the ability to assist and augment human decision-making in various domains. From healthcare to transportation, AI will play a significant role in providing recommendations, analyzing data, and helping us make informed choices. However, as we embrace the potential benefits of AI, we must also address the ethical considerations surrounding human autonomy.

One of the key ethical considerations is the impact of AI on personal choices. While AI can offer valuable insights and suggestions, it is crucial to maintain individuals' freedom to make autonomous decisions. AI systems should be designed to support human decision-making processes rather than replace or override them. Transparency will be essential, ensuring that individuals understand the influence and limitations of AI in their decision-making processes.

Privacy is another critical aspect when it comes to human autonomy and AI. As AI relies on vast amounts of data to operate effectively, safeguarding personal information will be paramount. Ethical frameworks will emphasize the need for strict data protection measures, ensuring that individuals have control over their personal data and are not subject to unwarranted surveillance or manipulation. Respecting privacy rights will be instrumental in preserving human autonomy and preventing the misuse of AI technologies.

Moreover, concerns may arise regarding the potential for undue influence from AI systems. In 2100, it will be crucial to establish safeguards and regulations that protect against the manipulation or coercion of individuals through AI. Ethical guidelines will ensure that AI systems are designed to empower individuals, providing them with unbiased information and options, rather than steering them towards predetermined outcomes or biases.

To address these ethical considerations, a multidisciplinary approach will be necessary. Collaboration between AI developers, ethicists, policymakers, and the wider public will be crucial in shaping the ethical frameworks that govern AI and human autonomy. Public dialogue and engagement will provide insights into societal values, concerns, and aspirations, ensuring that AI technologies align with our collective vision of human autonomy and well-being.

Additionally, education and awareness will play a vital role in empowering individuals to navigate the evolving landscape of AI and autonomy. Building digital literacy skills and promoting critical thinking will help individuals understand the capabilities and limitations of AI systems, enabling them to make informed decisions and exercise their autonomy effectively.

In conclusion, in 2100, it is essential to strike a balance between AI and human autonomy. Ethical frameworks and regulations will guide the development and deployment of AI technologies, ensuring that they respect and enhance human decision-making while safeguarding privacy and protecting against undue influence. Through interdisciplinary collaboration and public engagement, we can shape a future where AI empowers individuals, preserves human agency, and respects the fundamental principle of autonomy.

3.Bias and Fairness in AI Systems:

Addressing bias and ensuring fairness in AI systems will be a significant ethical concern in 2100. As AI algorithms make decisions that affect people's lives, it will be essential to identify and mitigate biases embedded in training data and algorithms. Efforts will be made to ensure diverse representation and inclusive practices during the development and testing of AI systems. Continuous monitoring and auditing will be necessary to detect and rectify biases that may emerge over time.

As AI algorithms increasingly make decisions that impact people's lives, it is crucial that we address biases and ensure fairness in these systems.

Bias in AI systems can arise from various sources, including biased training data, algorithmic design, and the context in which AI is deployed. Biased training data, which may reflect historical inequalities and social biases, can perpetuate and amplify discriminatory outcomes. In 2100, it will be crucial to identify and mitigate these biases to ensure fair and equitable AI systems.

To address bias, efforts will be made to ensure diverse representation and inclusive practices during the development and testing of AI systems. By involving a diverse group of stakeholders, including individuals from different cultural, ethnic, and socioeconomic backgrounds, we can minimize the risk of biased outcomes and ensure that AI technologies are inclusive and fair.

Moreover, continuous monitoring and auditing of AI systems will be necessary to detect and rectify biases that may emerge over time. This includes regularly reviewing and updating training data, evaluating algorithmic performance, and conducting impact assessments to identify any disparate impacts on different groups. By proactively monitoring for bias, we can take corrective measures to mitigate its effects and promote fairness in AI systems.

Transparency will also play a crucial role in addressing bias and ensuring fairness. AI algorithms should be designed in a transparent manner, enabling users and stakeholders to understand how decisions are being made. Transparent AI systems will allow for scrutiny and accountability, fostering trust and providing opportunities to identify and rectify any biases that may exist.

Furthermore, it is important to foster collaboration between AI developers, ethicists, policymakers, and affected communities to collectively address bias and fairness in AI systems. This collaboration will ensure that a diverse range of perspectives are considered, and that decisions regarding bias mitigation are made collectively. By fostering inclusive dialogue and engaging with impacted communities, we can better understand their concerns and develop effective strategies to address bias and ensure fairness.

In conclusion, addressing bias and ensuring fairness in AI systems will be a significant ethical concern in 2100. By promoting diverse representation, continuous monitoring, transparency, and collaboration, we can work towards developing AI technologies that are unbiased, fair, and promote equal opportunities for all. Let us strive for a future where AI systems contribute to a more equitable and just society.

4.AI in Governance and Decision-making:

In 2100, AI will play a role in governance and decision-making processes. Ethical considerations will arise around the use of AI in policy formulation, resource allocation, and public service delivery. Transparency, accountability, and public participation will be crucial to ensure that AI systems are used for the collective benefit of society, and that decisions made by AI systems align with societal values and goals.

As AI technologies continue to advance, they will undoubtedly have an impact on various aspects of governance, including policy formulation, resource allocation, and public service delivery. However, it is essential to consider the ethical implications that arise from the use of AI in these processes.

In 2100, AI systems will have the potential to enhance the efficiency, accuracy, and effectiveness of decision-making in governance. These systems can analyze vast amounts of data, identify patterns, and provide insights that can inform policy formulation and resource allocation. AI can help governments make evidence-based decisions, anticipate emerging issues, and respond proactively to societal challenges.

However, as we integrate AI into governance processes, it is crucial to address ethical considerations to ensure that AI is used for the collective benefit of society. Transparency and accountability will be essential principles guiding the use of AI in governance. The decision-making processes involving AI should be transparent, allowing for scrutiny and understanding of how decisions are made. This transparency will build trust and allow citizens to hold decision-makers accountable for the outcomes of AI-driven governance.

Public participation will also be crucial in shaping AI-driven governance. The involvement of citizens and stakeholders in the design and implementation of AI systems can help ensure that the technology aligns with societal values, goals, and aspirations. By engaging the public, governments can address concerns, mitigate biases, and ensure that AI systems reflect the diversity of perspectives and needs of the communities they serve.

Another ethical consideration in AI-driven governance is the potential for unintended consequences and bias. AI algorithms are trained on historical data, which may contain biases and inequalities. If not addressed, these biases can perpetuate and amplify societal inequalities. Therefore, it is essential to continuously monitor and evaluate AI systems to identify and mitigate biases that may emerge over time. The responsible and ethical use of AI in governance requires ongoing scrutiny and assessment to ensure fairness and equal opportunities for all.

Furthermore, safeguards should be put in place to protect privacy and ensure data security in AI-driven governance. As AI systems rely on vast amounts of data, it is crucial to protect individuals' privacy rights and prevent misuse or unauthorized access to sensitive information. Robust data protection measures and legal frameworks will be necessary to safeguard individual rights and maintain public trust in AI-driven governance.

as AI becomes increasingly integrated into governance and decision-making processes in 2100, it is important to address ethical considerations. Transparency, accountability, public participation, and the mitigation of biases will be critical to ensure that AI is used to benefit society as a whole. By fostering inclusive dialogue and adopting responsible practices, we can harness the potential of AI to make more informed and equitable decisions, ultimately improving the lives of citizens.

5.AI and Employment Disruption:

The widespread adoption of AI in various industries will raise concerns about its impact on employment in 2100. Ethical considerations will center on issues such as job displacement, income inequality, and re-skilling of the workforce. Strategies will be devised to manage the transition, ensuring that the benefits of AI are shared equitably and that support mechanisms are in place to assist individuals affected by automation.

As AI technologies continue to advance, concerns arise regarding job displacement, income inequality, and the need for re-skilling the workforce. It is crucial to address these ethical considerations and develop strategies to manage the transition in a way that benefits society as a whole.

The widespread adoption of AI in various industries will undoubtedly lead to automation and the displacement of certain jobs. While AI has the potential to improve efficiency, productivity, and innovation, it may also render certain tasks and roles obsolete. This disruption can create anxiety and uncertainty among workers, as they face the possibility of unemployment or the need to transition to new occupations.

To address this disruption, it is essential to develop strategies that ensure the benefits of AI are shared equitably. This means considering measures such as income redistribution, social safety nets, and upskilling programs. By redistributing the gains from AI adoption, we can mitigate the negative impact on those affected by job displacement and income inequality.

Additionally, re-skilling and lifelong learning initiatives will be crucial in preparing the workforce for the jobs of the future. As automation takes over routine and repetitive tasks, there will be a growing demand for skills that are uniquely human, such as critical thinking, creativity, emotional intelligence, and problem-solving. Governments, educational institutions, and businesses must collaborate to provide accessible and comprehensive re-training programs that equip individuals with the skills needed to thrive in an AI-driven economy.

Moreover, as we navigate the impact of AI on employment, it is vital to consider the potential societal benefits that AI can bring. By automating mundane and repetitive tasks, AI can free up human potential for more meaningful and fulfilling work. It can unlock new opportunities for innovation, entrepreneurship, and job creation in emerging fields related to AI development, maintenance, and ethics.

Ethical considerations surrounding AI and employment disruption also extend to issues of fairness and bias. AI algorithms are only as good as the data they are trained on, and if that data is biased, it can perpetuate existing inequalities and biases in hiring, promotion, and decision-making processes. Ensuring fairness and equity in AI-driven employment practices will require ongoing monitoring, evaluation, and the development of guidelines and regulations to prevent discrimination and bias.

as AI becomes increasingly integrated into various industries in 2100, ethical considerations regarding employment disruption are of paramount importance. Strategies to manage the transition, redistribute the benefits, and provide support to affected individuals are crucial for a just and equitable society. By focusing on re-skilling, lifelong learning, and fostering an inclusive and supportive environment, we can harness the potential of AI to create new opportunities and ensure a prosperous future for all.

6.AI and Privacy:

In 2100, the extensive use of AI will give rise to privacy concerns. Ethical considerations will revolve around data collection, storage, and usage. Striking a balance between utilizing personal data for AI advancements and protecting individuals' privacy rights will be crucial. Stringent privacy regulations and robust data protection mechanisms will be implemented to ensure that AI systems operate within ethical boundaries and respect individuals' privacy.

. As AI technologies continue to advance and become more integrated into our lives, ethical considerations surrounding data collection, storage, and usage become paramount. Striking a balance between utilizing personal data for AI advancements and safeguarding individuals' privacy rights will be crucial in shaping a responsible and ethical AI-driven society.

The growth of AI relies heavily on data, and as AI systems become more sophisticated, they require vast amounts of personal information to train and operate effectively. However, this collection of personal data raises significant concerns about privacy. Individuals must have confidence that their personal information is handled responsibly, transparently, and with their explicit consent.

To address these concerns, stringent privacy regulations and robust data protection mechanisms will be put in place. Governments, organizations, and AI developers will have a responsibility to adhere to ethical guidelines that prioritize privacy as a fundamental right. These guidelines should outline clear rules and procedures for data collection, ensuring that personal information is used only for specific, lawful purposes, and that data retention periods are limited.

Transparency and informed consent will be key principles in maintaining privacy in an AI-driven world. Individuals must have a clear understanding of what data is being collected, how it will be used, and who will have access to it. Privacy policies should be easily accessible, written in plain language, and provide individuals with meaningful control over their personal data. AI systems should also be designed to minimize the collection and storage of unnecessary personal information, adhering to the principles of data minimization and purpose limitation.

Furthermore, technological advancements in encryption and anonymization techniques will play a vital role in protecting privacy. By implementing strong encryption methods, sensitive personal data can be securely transmitted and stored, ensuring that unauthorized access is prevented. Anonymization techniques can also be employed to remove personally identifiable information, allowing for the analysis of data without compromising individual privacy.

Ethical considerations surrounding AI and privacy also extend to the responsible use of personal data. AI algorithms must be designed to respect privacy and avoid discriminatory or intrusive practices. It is essential to prevent the misuse of personal data for surveillance, profiling, or any other unethical purposes. Regular audits and oversight mechanisms should be in place to ensure compliance with privacy regulations and to hold accountable those who violate privacy rights.

in the year 2100, as AI becomes an integral part of our lives, ethical considerations regarding privacy will be crucial. Robust privacy regulations, transparency, informed consent, and responsible data practices will be necessary to protect individuals' privacy rights. By prioritizing privacy and implementing strong safeguards, we can foster trust, respect individual autonomy, and ensure that the benefits of AI are realized in a manner that respects and protects our fundamental right to privacy.

7.AI and Accountability:

As AI systems become more autonomous, the question of accountability will be paramount. Ethical frameworks will be developed to attribute responsibility when AI systems make decisions or engage in actions with significant consequences. The allocation of accountability among AI developers, users, and regulatory bodies will be explored, ensuring that ethical guidelines and legal frameworks address issues of liability and accountability.

As AI systems become more autonomous and capable of making decisions that impact our lives, ethical considerations surrounding accountability arise. It becomes crucial to develop frameworks that attribute responsibility when AI systems engage in actions or make decisions with significant consequences.

When AI systems operate autonomously, the traditional understanding of accountability becomes more complex. The question of who should be held accountable for the actions or decisions of AI systems requires careful consideration. Ethical frameworks will be developed to address this challenge and ensure that accountability is properly allocated.

First and foremost, accountability lies with the developers and creators of AI systems. These individuals and organizations have a responsibility to design and train AI systems that operate ethically and within legal boundaries. They must consider the potential consequences of their creations and implement mechanisms to ensure transparency, fairness, and safety.

Users of AI systems also bear a level of accountability. While developers provide the tools and frameworks, users must employ AI systems responsibly and in accordance with ethical guidelines. They should ensure that the data used to train AI models is unbiased and representative, and they should regularly evaluate the performance and potential biases of AI systems.

Regulatory bodies and policymakers play a crucial role in establishing legal frameworks and guidelines for AI accountability. They will have the responsibility to define the boundaries within which AI systems can operate, set standards for transparency and fairness, and ensure that appropriate mechanisms are in place to address ethical concerns and violations.

In the future, ethical guidelines and legal frameworks will be instrumental in addressing issues of liability and accountability. These frameworks should outline the responsibilities of AI developers, users, and regulatory bodies, defining the conditions under which each party should be held accountable for the actions and decisions of AI systems. It is essential to strike a balance between innovation and accountability, allowing for the advancement of AI while safeguarding against potential harm.

Moreover, efforts should be made to ensure transparency and explainability of AI systems. This means that AI algorithms should be designed in a way that enables humans to understand the reasoning behind their decisions. This transparency will not only enhance accountability but also foster trust and enable individuals to challenge and correct any biases or errors that may arise.

AI systems become more autonomous, accountability becomes a critical ethical consideration. By developing ethical frameworks, allocating responsibility among developers, users, and regulatory bodies, and promoting transparency and explainability, we can establish a robust accountability system for AI. Striking the right balance between innovation and accountability is vital to ensure that AI technologies are developed and deployed in a responsible and beneficial manner.

In 2100, the ethical considerations surrounding AI will be central to its responsible and beneficial deployment. Robust ethical frameworks, transparency, fairness, human autonomy, privacy protection, and accountability will guide the development and use of AI systems. By navigating the complexities of AI and ethics, society can harness the transformative potential of AI while upholding fundamental values, safeguarding human well-being, and promoting a future where AI technologies serve the best interests of humanity as a whole.

16

Bioethics in an Era of Genetic Engineering

The year 2100 presents a world where genetic engineering technologies have reached unparalleled levels of sophistication, offering unprecedented opportunities to modify and manipulate the human genome. As society delves into the realm of genetic engineering, ethical considerations become paramount. This chapter explores the landscape of bioethics in 2100, focusing on the challenges, dilemmas, and ethical frameworks that guide the responsible use of genetic engineering technologies.

1.Ethical Frameworks for Genetic Engineering:

In 2100, bioethics will provide the foundation for ethical decision-making in the field of genetic engineering. Robust frameworks will be developed, encompassing principles such as beneficence, non-maleficence, autonomy, justice, and respect for human dignity. These ethical frameworks will help navigate the complex landscape of genetic engineering and ensure responsible and ethical practices.

As advancements in genetic engineering continue to unfold, it is imperative that we establish robust ethical guidelines to guide our decisions and actions.

Genetic engineering holds immense potential for addressing various challenges in healthcare, agriculture, and environmental sustainability. However, with this immense power comes the responsibility to ensure that these advancements are pursued ethically and with respect for human dignity.

In the year 2100, bioethics will form the foundation for ethical decision-making in the realm of genetic engineering. These ethical frameworks will be designed to guide scientists, policymakers, and society as a whole in navigating the complex and sometimes controversial field.

One key principle that will underpin these ethical frameworks is beneficence, which emphasizes the importance of maximizing benefits and promoting the well-being of individuals and society. Genetic engineering should strive to alleviate suffering, treat diseases, and enhance human health while minimizing potential harm.

Non-maleficence, the principle of doing no harm, will also be paramount. The ethical frameworks will stress the importance of thoroughly assessing the risks and potential unintended consequences associated with genetic engineering. The goal will be to ensure that any interventions are safe and do not result in unforeseen negative impacts on individuals, communities, or the environment.

Autonomy, the principle that upholds an individual's right to make informed decisions about their own genetic makeup, will be another core element of these ethical frameworks. Respecting the autonomy of individuals and providing them with accurate and comprehensive information will be essential in promoting responsible and ethical practices in genetic engineering.

Justice will also play a central role. Ethical frameworks will emphasize the importance of ensuring equitable access to genetic technologies and their benefits. Genetic engineering should not exacerbate existing social disparities but rather strive to reduce inequalities and promote fairness in the distribution of resources and opportunities.

Lastly, these ethical frameworks will underscore the importance of respecting human dignity. Genetic engineering should never be used to discriminate, stigmatize, or devalue individuals based on their genetic makeup. Instead, it should empower individuals, respect their inherent worth, and promote the principles of inclusivity and respect for diversity.

In 2100, as genetic engineering continues to advance, ethical frameworks will serve as the compass that guides our actions. They will provide a set of principles to navigate the ethical challenges and dilemmas that arise in this field, ensuring that our scientific and technological progress is pursued in a responsible, respectful, and ethically sound manner.

By adhering to these ethical frameworks, we can harness the potential of genetic engineering to improve human health, enhance agricultural productivity, and address environmental challenges, all while upholding the values that define us as a compassionate and ethical society.

In conclusion, ethical frameworks in genetic engineering will be vital in shaping the future of this field in 2100. By embracing principles of beneficence, non-maleficence, autonomy, justice, and respect for human dignity, we can ensure that genetic engineering serves the betterment of humanity while maintaining a deep sense of responsibility and ethical integrity.

2.Informed Consent and Autonomy:

As genetic engineering technologies advance, the principle of informed consent and individual autonomy will become increasingly crucial. Individuals must have comprehensive knowledge and understanding of the potential risks, benefits, and implications of genetic interventions. Ethical guidelines will emphasize the importance of ensuring that individuals freely and voluntarily provide informed consent before undergoing any genetic modifications.

As advancements in genetic technologies continue to push the boundaries of scientific possibility, it is imperative that we prioritize these principles to uphold the rights and well-being of individuals.

In the year 2100, informed consent will serve as a cornerstone in the ethical practice of genetic engineering. This principle recognizes the autonomy and agency of individuals, empowering them to make informed decisions about their own genetic makeup and the potential interventions they may undergo.

Informed consent requires individuals to have a comprehensive understanding of the risks, benefits, and implications associated with genetic engineering. They must be provided with clear and accurate information about the nature of the intervention, its potential outcomes, and any potential risks or limitations involved.

Ethical guidelines will stress the importance of ensuring that individuals are not coerced or manipulated into consenting to genetic modifications. Consent must be freely given, without undue pressure or influence from external factors. This safeguards the integrity of the decision-making process and respects the autonomy of individuals.

Additionally, informed consent goes beyond a one-time decision. Individuals should have the right to change their minds and withdraw their consent at any stage of the genetic engineering process. Ongoing communication, support, and access to information are essential to ensure that individuals are empowered to make choices that align with their values and best interests.

Furthermore, ethical frameworks will emphasize the importance of considering the long-term consequences of genetic interventions. Individuals must be informed about potential impacts on their health, well-being, and the potential hereditary implications for future generations. By providing comprehensive information, individuals can make decisions that align with their personal values and aspirations.

In 2100, the principle of informed consent will be at the forefront of ethical practice in genetic engineering. It ensures that individuals are active participants in the decision-making process, fostering respect for their autonomy, values, and desires.

By prioritizing informed consent, we safeguard individual rights, promote transparency, and maintain ethical integrity. Genetic engineering technologies should be used to enhance individuals' lives while respecting their autonomy and right to make informed choices about their own genetic makeup.

In conclusion, in the realm of genetic engineering, informed consent and individual autonomy will be paramount in 2100. By upholding these principles, we can ensure that individuals have the necessary knowledge and agency to make decisions regarding their genetic interventions, fostering a culture of respect, transparency, and ethical responsibility.

3.Human Enhancement and Equality:

The advent of genetic engineering in 2100 will raise questions about human enhancement and equality. Ethical considerations will revolve around the equitable distribution of genetic interventions, preventing the exacerbation of existing inequalities, and avoiding the creation of a genetically divided society. Ensuring that access to genetic enhancements is fair and does not further marginalize certain groups will be a key ethical challenge.

As advancements in genetic technologies continue to unlock new possibilities, we must carefully consider the ethical implications of using these technologies to enhance human capabilities.

In an ideal world, the benefits of genetic enhancements would be accessible to all individuals, regardless of their socioeconomic background or other personal circumstances. However, as we have seen throughout history, technological advancements have often led to the exacerbation of existing inequalities. Therefore, in the year 2100, it is crucial that we approach the issue of human enhancement with a strong commitment to equality and social justice.

One of the key ethical considerations in human enhancement will be ensuring that access to genetic interventions is distributed in a fair and equitable manner. We must guard against the creation of a genetically divided society, where only a privileged few have access to the benefits of genetic enhancements while others are left behind.

To address this challenge, ethical frameworks will be developed to guide the distribution and accessibility of genetic interventions. These frameworks will emphasize the need to prioritize marginalized communities and individuals who may be disadvantaged due to socioeconomic factors, disabilities, or other circumstances. Efforts will be made to prevent further marginalization and to ensure that genetic enhancements do not widen existing inequalities.

Another crucial aspect of promoting equality in human enhancement is the avoidance of genetic determinism. Ethical guidelines will stress the importance of recognizing and valuing the inherent worth and dignity of every individual, regardless of their genetic makeup. Genetic enhancements should not be used to devalue or discriminate against those who do not possess certain desired traits or capabilities.

Furthermore, ethical considerations will involve engaging in inclusive dialogue and decision-making processes. It is essential to involve diverse voices and perspectives in shaping the policies and regulations surrounding human enhancement. This will help prevent biases and ensure that the interests and values of all individuals are taken into account.

In 2100, human enhancement technologies should be approached in a manner that upholds the principles of equality, fairness, and social justice. By proactively addressing the potential inequalities that may arise, we can work towards a future where access to genetic enhancements is not limited to a privileged few, but is available to all individuals, regardless of their backgrounds or circumstances.

In conclusion, as we navigate the exciting possibilities of genetic engineering in 2100, we must ensure that the pursuit of human enhancement is firmly rooted in the principles of equality and fairness. By addressing the challenges of distribution, avoiding genetic determinism, and fostering inclusive decision-making processes, we can strive towards a future where genetic enhancements contribute to a more equitable and just society for all.

4.Germline Editing and Inherited Modifications:

The ability to modify the germline, affecting future generations, presents unique ethical dilemmas. In 2100, discussions surrounding the ethical boundaries of germline editing will be prominent. Questions of safety, unintended consequences, and the potential for irreversibility will need to be carefully considered. Ethical guidelines will be established to ensure responsible use and governance of germline editing technologies.

As genetic technologies continue to advance, the ability to modify the germline, affecting future generations, presents us with unique and complex ethical dilemmas.

Germline editing involves making changes to the DNA of reproductive cells, such as sperm and eggs, which can result in inherited modifications that are passed down to future generations. This ability to alter the genetic makeup of our descendants raises profound ethical considerations that demand our careful attention.

First and foremost, the safety and well-being of individuals must be at the forefront of any ethical discussions surrounding germline editing. Given the potential for unintended consequences and unforeseen risks, it is crucial that rigorous scientific research and testing be conducted to ensure the safety and effectiveness of germline editing technologies. Ethical guidelines and regulations will be established to ensure responsible and accountable use, ensuring that any modifications made to the germline are done with the utmost caution and consideration for the potential impact on future generations.

Furthermore, the irreversibility of germline modifications poses another significant ethical challenge. Once changes are made to the germline, they become a permanent part of an individual's genetic inheritance, affecting not only that person but also all future generations. This raises questions about consent and the rights of individuals who have yet to be born. Ethical frameworks will be developed to navigate these complex issues, ensuring that decisions regarding germline editing are made with careful consideration of the long-term consequences and the potential impacts on future individuals.

In addition to safety and irreversibility, questions of equity and justice will also emerge. It will be essential to address concerns regarding the equitable access to germline editing technologies, ensuring that they are not limited to a privileged few but are made available in a fair and inclusive manner. Ethical guidelines will be established to prevent the exacerbation of existing social and economic disparities and to promote equal opportunities for all individuals.

Importantly, discussions surrounding germline editing must involve a wide range of stakeholders, including scientists, ethicists, policymakers, and the public. Open and transparent dialogue will be essential to ensure that diverse perspectives are considered, and decisions are made in the best interest of society as a whole.

In conclusion, in 2100, the ethical boundaries of germline editing will be at the forefront of discussions surrounding genetic technologies. The safety, unintended consequences, and irreversibility of germline modifications will require careful consideration and adherence to robust ethical guidelines. By promoting responsible use, prioritizing safety, and addressing concerns of equity and justice, we can navigate the ethical complexities of germline editing and ensure that these technologies are employed in a manner that respects the well-being and rights of all individuals, present and future.

5.Genetic Privacy and Discrimination:

As genetic information becomes more accessible and widely used, concerns about privacy and genetic discrimination will be significant ethical considerations. Safeguarding genetic privacy and preventing the misuse of genetic information will be crucial to protect individuals from discrimination based on their genetic profiles. Ethical guidelines and legal frameworks will be developed to ensure the responsible handling and protection of genetic data.

As advances in genetic technologies continue to unfold, the accessibility and utilization of genetic information will raise significant ethical considerations that we must address with great care.

With the increasing availability of genetic testing and personalized medicine, individuals have greater access to their own genetic information than ever before. While this knowledge can provide valuable insights into our health and well-being, it also raises concerns about the privacy and security of our genetic data.

Genetic privacy is a fundamental human right that should be protected and respected. Genetic information is deeply personal, containing intimate details about our health, ancestry, and predispositions to certain conditions. As we move forward, it is essential that robust ethical guidelines and legal frameworks be established to safeguard the privacy of individuals' genetic data.

Moreover, the potential for genetic discrimination poses a significant ethical challenge. Genetic information can be misused to discriminate against individuals in various aspects of life, including employment, insurance coverage, and access to education or other opportunities. Discrimination based on genetic profiles undermines the principles of equality and fairness, and it can have far-reaching consequences for individuals and their families.

To address these concerns, ethical guidelines and legal protections will be developed to ensure the responsible handling and protection of genetic information. Measures will be put in place to prevent unauthorized access, misuse, or discrimination based on genetic data. Transparency and informed consent will be emphasized to ensure that individuals have control over how their genetic information is used and shared.

In addition to legal safeguards, public awareness and education will play a crucial role in promoting responsible practices and combating genetic discrimination. Educating individuals about the importance of genetic privacy, the potential risks of genetic discrimination, and their rights regarding their genetic data will empower them to make informed decisions and protect their privacy.

Furthermore, collaboration between policymakers, healthcare providers, researchers, and industry stakeholders will be essential to develop comprehensive approaches that balance the benefits of genetic information with the need for privacy protection. Ethical considerations and stakeholder engagement should guide the development of policies and practices that strike a balance between the potential benefits of genetic information and the protection of individual rights.

In conclusion, in 2100, genetic privacy and the prevention of genetic discrimination will be significant ethical concerns. Safeguarding the privacy of genetic data and preventing the misuse of genetic information will be essential to protect individuals' rights and ensure fairness and equality in society. Through the establishment of ethical guidelines, legal protections, public awareness, and collaboration between stakeholders, we can create a future in which individuals can benefit from genetic advancements while preserving their privacy and protecting themselves from discrimination.

6.Long-term Consequences and Environmental Impacts:

Genetic engineering interventions may have long-term consequences and potential environmental impacts. In 2100, ethical considerations will include evaluating the potential ecological effects of genetically modified organisms and mitigating any risks to biodiversity. Precautionary measures, environmental assessments, and responsible stewardship will guide the ethical use of genetic engineering technologies to minimize harm to ecosystems.

As we explore the potential of genetic engineering to transform various aspects of our lives, it is crucial that we assess and address the potential ecological effects and mitigate any risks to biodiversity.

Genetic engineering has the power to modify organisms at the genetic level, offering immense possibilities for improving agricultural productivity, enhancing disease resistance, and addressing pressing environmental challenges. However, we must be mindful of the potential long-term consequences and unintended environmental impacts that these interventions may have.

In the pursuit of advancements, it is essential to adopt a precautionary approach. We must carefully consider the potential risks and uncertainties associated with genetically modified organisms (GMOs) before introducing them into the environment. This means conducting thorough environmental assessments and research to understand the potential ecological effects of genetic engineering interventions.

Preserving biodiversity is of utmost importance. Genetic modifications that are intended to provide benefits should not come at the expense of jeopardizing the delicate balance of ecosystems or endangering native species. It is our responsibility to ensure that any genetic engineering interventions are guided by responsible stewardship and are designed to minimize harm to ecosystems.

Ethical guidelines will be essential in guiding the ethical use of genetic engineering technologies. These guidelines will emphasize the importance of long-term monitoring, impact assessment, and the ongoing evaluation of the environmental consequences of genetic modifications. This will help us detect and mitigate any unforeseen risks that may emerge over time.

Collaboration and knowledge-sharing among scientists, environmentalists, policymakers, and communities will be crucial. By fostering interdisciplinary dialogue and involving stakeholders in decision-making processes, we can ensure that genetic engineering interventions are not only scientifically sound but also ethically responsible and environmentally sustainable.

In addition, transparency and public engagement will be vital in fostering trust and understanding. Public discussions and debates on the potential environmental impacts of genetic engineering will enable us to consider diverse perspectives, ethical concerns, and societal values in shaping the direction of research, regulation, and implementation.

As we navigate the possibilities of genetic engineering in the future, we must keep in mind that our actions today can have lasting implications for the environment and future generations. By adopting a precautionary approach, conducting thorough assessments, and actively mitigating risks, we can harness the potential of genetic engineering while preserving the delicate balance of our ecosystems.

In conclusion, in 2100, ethical considerations will encompass the evaluation of long-term consequences and environmental impacts of genetic engineering interventions. We must exercise responsible stewardship, conduct thorough assessments, and adhere to ethical guidelines to minimize harm to ecosystems and preserve biodiversity. By fostering collaboration, transparency, and public engagement, we can ensure that genetic engineering is pursued in an environmentally responsible and ethically sound manner.

7.Global Collaboration and Governance:

Given the global nature of genetic engineering, international collaboration and governance will be essential. Ethical considerations will involve establishing global standards, guidelines, and regulations to ensure the responsible use of genetic engineering technologies across nations. Collaborative efforts will focus on fostering transparency, sharing best practices, and addressing ethical concerns in a coordinated manner.

In 2100, bioethics will play a central role in guiding the responsible use of genetic engineering technologies. Ethical frameworks encompassing informed consent, autonomy, equality, privacy, and environmental stewardship will help navigate the complex ethical considerations surrounding genetic engineering. By striking a balance between scientific progress and ethical considerations, society can harness the potential benefits of genetic engineering while upholding fundamental values, ensuring societal well-being, and promoting a future where genetic interventions serve the best interests of humanity and the environment.

VIII

Transforming Industries

17

Automation and the Future of Work

The year 2100 presents a world where automation and advanced technologies have reshaped the landscape of work and employment. As artificial intelligence, robotics, and automation continue to advance, the future of work undergoes significant transformations. This chapter explores the implications of automation on the future of work in 2100, examining the challenges, opportunities, and strategies for navigating this rapidly evolving labor market.

- **Technological Advancements and Automation:**

In 2100, automation technologies will have revolutionized various industries, leading to significant changes in the nature of work. Advanced robotics, AI-driven systems, and machine learning algorithms will automate routine tasks, augment human capabilities, and reshape job roles across sectors. The chapter explores the range of industries impacted by automation, including manufacturing, healthcare, transportation, and service sectors.

The rapid development of automation technologies, driven by robotics, artificial intelligence (AI), and machine learning, will bring forth a wave of transformative changes in the nature of work across various sectors.

Automation holds the promise of revolutionizing industries by automating routine and repetitive tasks, freeing up human potential for more creative and

193

complex endeavors. Advanced robotics will work alongside human workers, enhancing their capabilities and increasing productivity. AI-driven systems and machine learning algorithms will enable intelligent decision-making and streamline processes, leading to greater efficiency and innovation.

One of the sectors that will experience a profound impact is manufacturing. Automation technologies will enable the automation of assembly lines, reducing production costs, and increasing the speed and precision of manufacturing processes. This will not only improve productivity but also create safer working conditions for employees, as robots take over hazardous and physically demanding tasks.

The healthcare industry will also undergo significant transformation. AI-powered diagnostic tools and robotics will enhance medical imaging, facilitate early detection of diseases, and assist in surgical procedures. Automation will enable healthcare professionals to focus more on patient care and complex decision-making, leading to improved healthcare outcomes and more personalized treatments.

Transportation is another sector that will witness substantial changes. Self-driving vehicles will become commonplace, revolutionizing the way we commute and transport goods. Automation will lead to increased safety, reduced traffic congestion, and optimized logistics, resulting in more efficient and sustainable transportation systems.

Even the service sectors will not be immune to the impact of automation. AI-powered chatbots, virtual assistants, and automated customer service systems will provide efficient and personalized experiences for consumers. Automation will enable businesses to streamline their operations, deliver faster and more accurate services, and allocate resources more effectively.

However, as we embrace the potential of automation, we must also address the challenges it poses. The displacement of jobs and changes in the labor market will require proactive measures to ensure a smooth transition for workers. It will be crucial to invest in reskilling and upskilling programs to equip individuals with the necessary skills for the jobs of the future. Societies must also consider the social and economic implications of automation and work towards creating inclusive systems that benefit all.

Moreover, ethical considerations surrounding automation must be at the forefront of our discussions. We must ensure that the use of automation technologies aligns with our values, respects human dignity, and does not perpetuate inequalities. Responsible governance and regulations will be essential to address concerns such as privacy, algorithmic biases, and the responsible use of AI.

In conclusion, the year 2100 will witness remarkable technological advancements and automation across industries. While these developments offer immense potential for enhancing productivity, efficiency, and innovation, we must also address the challenges they pose. By investing in reskilling programs, fostering inclusive systems, and upholding ethical principles, we can navigate the transformative power of automation and ensure that its benefits are shared by all.

· **Evolving Job Roles and Skill Requirements:**

The automation-driven future of work will necessitate a shift in job roles and skill requirements. Repetitive and manual tasks will be largely automated, leading to a greater demand for skills such as creativity, critical thinking, complex problem-solving, and adaptability. The chapter examines the emerging job roles and the importance of lifelong learning and upskilling to thrive in a technologically advanced labor market.

As automation technologies continue to advance, they will redefine the landscape of the labor market, necessitating a shift in the types of jobs available and the skills required to thrive in this new era.

In the not-too-distant future, many routine and manual tasks will be automated, leading to a transformation in job roles across various industries. While this may raise concerns about job displacement, it also presents new opportunities for individuals to embrace more meaningful and fulfilling work.

The emergence of automation will create a demand for a new set of skills. Employers will increasingly seek individuals who possess skills that complement and augment the capabilities of automation technologies. Skills such as creativity, critical thinking, complex problem-solving, adaptability, emotional intelligence, and collaboration will be highly valued in this technologically advanced labor market.

Creativity will be vital as individuals will be required to think outside the box, come up with innovative solutions, and explore new possibilities. Critical thinking and complex problem-solving skills will be essential to analyze complex situations, identify patterns, and make informed decisions. The ability to adapt to new technologies, tools, and work environments will be crucial as automation continues to reshape industries at a rapid pace.

Emotional intelligence and interpersonal skills will become even more valuable in an automated world. As human interactions become increasingly important, individuals with the ability to empathize, communicate effectively, and build strong relationships will thrive. Collaboration and teamwork will be essential as individuals work alongside automation technologies and collaborate with diverse teams.

To navigate this shifting job landscape, lifelong learning and upskilling will be crucial. Individuals must be proactive in acquiring new knowledge, learning new skills, and staying abreast of the latest technological advancements. Lifelong learning will empower individuals to adapt to changing job requirements, explore new opportunities, and remain competitive in the labor market.

Businesses and educational institutions also have a crucial role to play in preparing individuals for the evolving job market. They must collaborate to develop educational programs and training initiatives that equip individuals with the necessary skills and competencies. This includes promoting interdisciplinary education, fostering entrepreneurship, and encouraging a culture of continuous learning.

It is important to recognize that this transition to an automated future will not happen overnight. It will be a gradual process that requires collective efforts from individuals, businesses, educational institutions, and policymakers. By embracing lifelong learning, fostering a culture of innovation, and investing in the development of future-proof skills, we can navigate this transformative period with confidence.

In conclusion, the automation-driven future of work will bring about a shift in job roles and skill requirements. As routine and manual tasks become automated, skills such as creativity, critical thinking, adaptability, and collaboration will be highly sought after. Lifelong learning and upskilling will be essential for individuals to thrive in this technologically advanced labor market. By embracing these changes and investing in our skills, we can embrace the opportunities presented by automation and shape a future where humans and technology work together harmoniously.

· **Impact on Employment and Economic Disruption:**

The widespread adoption of automation technologies will undoubtedly have an impact on employment and the economy. While automation can lead to job displacement in certain sectors, it also presents opportunities for new types of work and economic growth. The chapter delves into the potential effects on employment rates, income distribution, and the need for policies that address economic disruption and ensure a just transition.

· **Human-Machine Collaboration and Coexistence:**

In 2100, human-machine collaboration will be a critical aspect of the future of work. AI and automation will work alongside humans, augmenting their capabilities and improving productivity. Ethical considerations surrounding the interaction between humans and machines, including issues of decision-making authority, accountability, and the preservation of human dignity, will be explored.

As artificial intelligence and automation continue to advance, the interaction between humans and machines will become increasingly significant in our professional lives.

The future of work will see humans and machines working side by side, leveraging their respective strengths to achieve greater productivity, efficiency, and innovation. Machines, powered by artificial intelligence, will possess remarkable computational capabilities, enabling them to process vast amounts of data, analyze complex patterns, and perform repetitive tasks with speed and precision. Humans, on the other hand, bring unique qualities such as creativity, critical thinking, emotional intelligence, and ethical judgment to the table.

This collaboration between humans and machines will result in a synergy that surpasses what either party could achieve individually. Machines will augment human capabilities, allowing us to focus on higher-order tasks that require complex reasoning, creativity, and interpersonal skills. Through this collaboration, we can unleash the full potential of human ingenuity and leverage the power of technology to tackle complex challenges and drive innovation across industries.

However, as we embrace this era of human-machine collaboration, we must carefully consider the ethical implications and ensure that the relationship between humans and machines upholds our shared values and respects human dignity. Ethical considerations will revolve around decision-making authority, accountability, and the preservation of human autonomy.

When it comes to decision-making, it is essential to strike a balance between human judgment and machine-generated insights. While machines can provide valuable data-driven recommendations, the ultimate decision-making authority should rest with humans. It is crucial to retain human agency and ensure that ethical considerations, empathy, and social context are taken into account when making decisions that impact individuals and society as a whole.

Accountability is another crucial aspect of human-machine collaboration. While machines can execute tasks autonomously, humans must retain the responsibility and be accountable for the outcomes. Establishing clear lines of responsibility and accountability will be essential to address any unintended consequences or errors that may arise from the collaboration between humans and machines.

Preserving human dignity in the context of human-machine collaboration is of utmost importance. It is vital to ensure that individuals are not reduced to mere cogs in a machine-driven system. Respecting human dignity means designing technology and work processes that empower individuals, foster meaningful work, and prioritize their well-being. Additionally, measures must be in place to address potential biases, discrimination, and inequality that may emerge from automated systems.

To achieve a harmonious coexistence between humans and machines, it is crucial to invest in education and training. Developing digital literacy, computational thinking, and skills that complement AI and automation will enable individuals to adapt and thrive in this new era. Additionally, nurturing a culture that embraces lifelong learning, creativity, and adaptability will be crucial for individuals to navigate the evolving landscape of work.

In conclusion, human-machine collaboration and coexistence will shape the future of work in 2100. By harnessing the strengths of both humans and machines, we can achieve unprecedented levels of productivity, innovation, and societal progress. However, we must navigate this collaboration with careful ethical considerations, ensuring that decision-making authority rests with humans, accountability is maintained, and human dignity is preserved. Through thoughtful integration and a commitment to lifelong learning, we can create a future where humans and machines work together in harmony, unlocking the full potential of our collective intelligence.

- **Social Implications and Inequality:**

Automation in the labor market may exacerbate existing inequalities. The chapter addresses the potential social implications of automation, including income disparities, skills gaps, and access to employment opportunities.

Strategies to ensure inclusive growth, such as universal basic income, lifelong learning programs, and social safety nets, will be crucial in mitigating inequality and supporting individuals in the face of technological disruptions.

· Entrepreneurship and Innovation:

Automation in 2100 will also foster entrepreneurship and innovation. The chapter examines the opportunities for individuals to harness automation technologies to create new businesses, develop innovative solutions, and drive economic growth. The importance of fostering an entrepreneurial mindset, supporting startup ecosystems, and encouraging innovation will be explored.

· Redefining Work and Societal Values:

Automation in the future of work will require redefining societal values and our understanding of work. The chapter investigates the potential for a shift towards a more leisure-focused society, where individuals have more time for personal pursuits, creativity, and self-fulfillment. The implications for societal structures, cultural norms, and the well-being of individuals will be examined.

In 2100, automation will continue to shape the future of work, bringing about both challenges and opportunities. Navigating the transitions brought by automation will require strategic planning, investment in education and upskilling, social policies that address inequality, and a reevaluation of societal values. By embracing technological advancements, fostering human-machine collaboration, and prioritizing inclusivity, society can navigate the future of work in a way that ensures economic prosperity, social well-being, and meaningful human contributions in an automated world.

18

Energy Revolution and Clean Technologies

The year 2100 presents a world where the energy landscape has undergone a profound revolution, driven by the urgent need to combat climate change and ensure a sustainable future. This chapter explores the advancements and implications of clean technologies in 2100, examining the energy revolution and its transformative impact on society, economy, and the environment.

Renewable Energy Dominance:

By 2100, renewable energy sources will have become the dominant players in the global energy mix. The chapter explores the significant advancements in solar, wind, hydro, and geothermal technologies, their increased efficiency, and scalability. Renewable energy systems will be integrated into smart grids, enabling decentralized energy production and distribution, reducing reliance on fossil fuels, and mitigating greenhouse gas emissions.

I will share with you explores the remarkable advancements in solar, wind, hydro, and geothermal technologies that will drive this transformation.

In 2100, renewable energy will have become the go-to solution for meeting our energy needs. Solar power, derived from the infinite energy of the sun, will continue to thrive as technology advancements enhance the efficiency and affordability of solar panels. Large-scale solar farms and innovative solutions such as building-integrated photovoltaics will harness the power of sunlight, providing clean and abundant energy to homes, businesses, and industries.

Similarly, wind energy will soar to new heights, literally and figuratively. Advances in wind turbine technology will make wind farms more efficient and productive. Offshore wind farms, utilizing the vast wind resources of our oceans, will contribute significantly to the renewable energy revolution. With their ability to generate power even in challenging weather conditions, wind turbines will become an indispensable part of our energy infrastructure.

Hydropower, a tried and tested renewable energy source, will continue to play a crucial role in our energy transition. As we design and implement more sustainable hydropower systems, we will maximize energy generation while minimizing environmental impacts. From large-scale dams to run-of-river projects, hydropower will provide a reliable and clean source of electricity, helping to meet our growing energy demands.

Moreover, geothermal energy, tapping into the Earth's natural heat, will experience substantial growth. Geothermal power plants will harness the energy stored beneath our feet, providing a continuous and baseload source of clean energy. Advancements in drilling techniques and heat extraction technologies will unlock the full potential of geothermal energy, making it a key contributor to our renewable energy mix.

In addition to the advancements in renewable energy technologies themselves, the integration of these systems into smart grids will revolutionize our energy infrastructure. Smart grids will enable decentralized energy production, allowing individuals and communities to generate and share clean energy. Energy storage technologies, such as advanced batteries, will store excess energy for times when the sun isn't shining or the wind isn't blowing. This integration will ensure a reliable and stable energy supply while reducing our reliance on fossil fuels and mitigating greenhouse gas emissions.

The shift towards renewable energy dominance is not just a matter of environmental stewardship; it is also an economic opportunity. The renewable energy sector will create millions of jobs, driving economic growth and fostering innovation. Investments in research and development will spur breakthroughs in energy storage, grid optimization, and renewable energy technologies, further accelerating the clean energy revolution.

As we move towards a future powered by renewable energy, it is crucial to ensure a just and equitable transition. We must prioritize the inclusion of communities affected by the shift away from traditional energy sources, providing training and support for workers in fossil fuel industries to transition to renewable energy jobs. This transition presents an opportunity to address social and economic disparities, creating a more sustainable and fair society.

In conclusion, by 2100, renewable energy will dominate the global energy mix, revolutionizing the way we power our world. With advancements in solar, wind, hydro, and geothermal technologies, and the integration of smart grids, we will have a clean, reliable, and sustainable energy infras-tructure. The renewable energy revolution not only promises environmental benefits but also economic growth and social progress. Let us embrace this transformation and work together to create a brighter, cleaner, and more prosperous future for generations to come.

- **Energy Storage and Grid Technologies:**

The wide-scale adoption of renewable energy will necessitate advanced energy storage and grid technologies. In 2100, the chapter examines breakthroughs in energy storage, including advanced battery technologies, supercapacitors, and emerging technologies like hydrogen storage. Smart grids will enable efficient energy management, grid optimization, and bidi-rectional energy flow, facilitating the integration of intermittent renewable sources into the energy infrastructure.

I will share with you explores the remarkable breakthroughs in energy storage and the evolution of smart grids that will underpin the widespread adoption of renewable energy sources.

As renewable energy becomes the dominant force in our energy mix, we must address the intermittent nature of sources like solar and wind power. Energy storage technologies will play a crucial role in bridging the gap between energy generation and consumption, ensuring a reliable and uninterrupted power supply.

Advanced battery technologies will be at the forefront of energy storage solutions. Breakthroughs in materials, design, and manufacturing processes will result in batteries that are more efficient, longer-lasting, and capable of storing larger amounts of energy. These advancements will make batteries an essential component of our energy infrastructure, enabling us to store excess renewable energy during times of low demand and release it when needed.

Supercapacitors, with their high power density and rapid charging capabilities, will complement batteries in providing instantaneous bursts of energy. Their ability to charge and discharge quickly will be crucial in meeting peak energy demands and stabilizing the grid during fluctuations.

In addition to batteries and supercapacitors, emerging energy storage technologies like hydrogen storage will play a significant role. Hydrogen, obtained through electrolysis using excess renewable energy, can be stored and converted back into electricity when needed. Its versatility and ability to store large amounts of energy make it a promising candidate for long-term energy storage and grid balancing.

Furthermore, the evolution of smart grids will revolutionize our energy infrastructure. Smart grids will enable efficient energy management and bidirectional energy flow, allowing for the integration of distributed energy sources such as rooftop solar panels and small wind turbines. These grids will incorporate advanced sensors, communication systems, and control mechanisms, optimizing energy distribution and reducing transmission losses.

By utilizing artificial intelligence and machine learning algorithms, smart grids will make real-time decisions based on data from various energy sources and consumer demand patterns. This dynamic and adaptive approach will enhance the efficiency and stability of the grid, enabling seamless integration of intermittent renewable energy sources.

Moreover, smart grids will facilitate demand response programs, empowering consumers to actively participate in energy management. Through smart meters and real-time energy consumption information, individuals and businesses will have the ability to adjust their energy usage, reduce peak demand, and contribute to a more balanced and sustainable grid.

The integration of electric vehicle (EV) charging infrastructure into smart grids will also play a significant role. EVs will not only serve as a means of transportation but also as mobile energy storage units. During times of high demand, EVs can feed excess energy back into the grid, supporting grid stability and reducing the need for additional power plants.

As we advance into the future, energy storage and smart grid technologies will be instrumental in maximizing the potential of renewable energy sources. The combination of advanced batteries, supercapacitors, hydrogen storage, and intelligent grid systems will ensure a reliable, resilient, and sustainable energy infrastructure.

However, we must also address the challenges associated with these technologies. Research and development efforts should focus on enhancing energy storage efficiency, extending the lifespan of batteries, and exploring novel storage solutions. Collaboration between governments, industries, and research institutions will be crucial to drive innovation and scale up these technologies.

In conclusion, in 2100, energy storage and grid technologies will play a pivotal role in harnessing the full potential of renewable energy sources. Advanced batteries, supercapacitors, hydrogen storage, and smart grid systems will enable us to achieve a reliable and resilient energy infrastructure. Let us embrace these technologies, invest in research and development, and work together to build a sustainable future powered by clean and renewable energy.

- **Electrification of Transportation:**

By 2100, transportation will be revolutionized by the electrification of vehicles. The chapter explores the advancements in electric vehicle (EV) technologies, including improved battery performance, ultra-fast charging infrastructure, and autonomous driving capabilities. The widespread adoption of EVs will reduce dependence on fossil fuel-powered vehicles, leading to significant emissions reductions and improved air quality.

I will share with you explores the remarkable advancements in electric vehicle technologies, the infrastructure supporting them, and the profound positive impacts they will have on our environment.

The electrification of transportation is set to revolutionize how we move people and goods. The development of electric vehicles (EVs) will lead to a significant reduction in our dependence on fossil fuel-powered vehicles, bringing forth a cleaner, greener, and more sustainable future.

One of the key advancements driving the electrification of transportation is the improvement in battery performance. In 2100, batteries will be more efficient, have higher energy densities, and longer lifespans. These advancements will enable EVs to achieve longer driving ranges and shorter charging times, making them a viable and convenient option for everyday use.

Ultra-fast charging infrastructure will also be in place to support the widespread adoption of EVs. Charging stations capable of replenishing the battery of an electric vehicle in a matter of minutes will be commonplace, reducing charging time to a level comparable to refueling a conventional vehicle with gasoline. This infrastructure will alleviate range anxiety and provide drivers with the confidence that they can travel long distances without compromising convenience.

Furthermore, the integration of autonomous driving capabilities in EVs will redefine the way we perceive transportation. Self-driving technologies will enhance safety, improve traffic flow, and optimize energy efficiency. Autonomous electric vehicles will be able to communicate with each other and the infrastructure, enabling seamless coordination and reducing congestion on our roads.

The electrification of transportation will have a profound impact on our environment. By transitioning from fossil fuel-powered vehicles to EVs, we will significantly reduce greenhouse gas emissions and combat climate change. The shift towards renewable energy sources to power these vehicles will ensure that their operation is virtually emission-free. Cleaner air, improved public health, and reduced noise pollution will be among the immediate benefits enjoyed by communities worldwide.

However, the successful electrification of transportation will require collective efforts and investments. Governments, industries, and individuals must work together to expand the charging infrastructure, develop supportive policies, and promote consumer adoption of EVs. Collaboration between the public and private sectors will be crucial in advancing battery technologies, driving down costs, and improving the overall performance of electric vehicles.

Moreover, the electrification of transportation opens up new opportunities for energy integration. EVs can serve as mobile energy storage units, allowing for bidirectional energy flow between the vehicle and the grid. During times of high demand, EVs can supply electricity back to the grid, supporting grid stability and optimizing energy distribution. This vehicle-to-grid integration will enable a more efficient and resilient energy system.

In conclusion, by 2100, the electrification of transportation will have transformed our mobility landscape. Electric vehicles with improved battery performance, ultra-fast charging infrastructure, and autonomous driving capabilities will be the new norm. The widespread adoption of EVs will reduce our reliance on fossil fuels, cut emissions, and enhance the quality of our environment. Let us embrace this transformation, invest in the necessary infrastructure, and accelerate the transition to a cleaner and more sustainable transportation system.

- **Sustainable Buildings and Smart Cities:**

In 2100, sustainable buildings and smart cities will be at the forefront of urban development. The chapter examines the integration of clean technologies into building design, such as energy-efficient materials, advanced insulation, and smart energy management systems. Smart cities will leverage IoT technologies, real-time data analytics, and AI-driven systems to optimize energy usage, reduce waste, and enhance quality of life.

In the year 2100, our cities will be transformed into vibrant and environmentally friendly spaces that prioritize energy efficiency, resource optimization, and a high quality of life for their residents.

The chapter I will share with you explores the integration of clean technologies into building design and the emergence of smart cities empowered by the Internet of Things (IoT), real-time data analytics, and AI-driven systems.

In 2100, sustainable buildings will set a new standard for construction. Energy-efficient materials, advanced insulation, and innovative designs will ensure that buildings minimize energy consumption while maximizing comfort. These structures will leverage renewable energy sources, such as solar panels and wind turbines, to generate clean electricity on-site. Additionally, green roofs and vertical gardens will enhance air quality, reduce the urban heat island effect, and provide spaces for urban agriculture.

But it doesn't stop there. Smart energy management systems will be an integral part of sustainable buildings. These systems will optimize energy usage by monitoring and adjusting lighting, heating, and cooling based on real-time data and occupant preferences. Energy-efficient appliances and smart meters will provide individuals with greater control over their energy consumption, promoting conscious energy use and reducing waste.

Furthermore, the concept of smart cities will transform the way we live and interact with our urban environments. IoT technologies will enable seamless connectivity between various aspects of urban life. Real-time data analytics will empower city authorities to make informed decisions regarding infrastructure, transportation, and public services.

AI-driven systems will play a crucial role in optimizing the functioning of smart cities. Traffic management systems will dynamically adjust traffic flow based on real-time data, reducing congestion and improving transportation efficiency. Waste management systems will employ sensors and automation to optimize collection routes, minimize waste generation, and enhance recycling rates. Intelligent lighting systems will adapt to the presence of individuals, reducing energy consumption without compromising safety.

Smart cities will also prioritize the well-being of their inhabitants. Sensor-equipped parks and public spaces will provide real-time air quality monitoring, ensuring that residents can enjoy a healthy environment. Advanced healthcare systems will leverage data analytics and telemedicine technologies to improve healthcare access and quality. Additionally, smart education systems will enhance learning experiences and foster knowledge sharing among individuals.

However, the development of sustainable buildings and smart cities requires collective efforts and partnerships. Governments, city planners, architects, and technology providers must collaborate to create supportive policies, invest in infrastructure, and foster innovation. Engaging citizens in the process, ensuring inclusivity, and addressing potential privacy and security concerns are also vital to the success of smart cities.

In conclusion, by 2100, sustainable buildings and smart cities will reshape our urban landscapes. Buildings will be designed to minimize energy consumption, harness renewable energy, and provide optimal living conditions. Smart cities will leverage technology to optimize energy usage, enhance infrastructure, and improve the quality of life for their residents. Let us embrace this vision of a sustainable and intelligent future, working together to build cities that are not only environmentally friendly but also nurturing and prosperous for all.

· **Decentralized Energy Generation:**

Advancements in clean technologies will enable decentralized energy generation in 2100. The chapter explores the rise of distributed energy systems, including rooftop solar panels, microgrids, and community-based energy initiatives. Decentralized energy generation will empower communities, enhance energy resilience, and enable energy access in remote areas, reducing dependence on centralized power grids and increasing energy equity.

In the year 2100, we will witness a remarkable transformation in the way we produce and consume energy, thanks to advancements in clean technologies and the rise of decentralized energy generation.

The chapter I will share with you explores the concept of decentralized energy generation and its profound impact on communities and the energy landscape.

In 2100, decentralized energy generation will revolutionize the way we power our homes, businesses, and communities. This shift will be driven by various clean technologies, including rooftop solar panels, microgrids, and community-based energy initiatives.

Rooftop solar panels will become ubiquitous, adorning homes and buildings, converting sunlight into clean electricity. This decentralized approach allows individuals and businesses to generate their own power, reducing reliance on traditional centralized power grids. Excess energy can be stored in advanced battery systems or fed back into the grid for others to utilize, promoting energy sharing and collaboration within communities.

Microgrids will play a pivotal role in decentralized energy generation. These localized grids connect multiple energy sources, such as solar panels, wind turbines, and energy storage systems, to serve specific areas or neighborhoods. By operating independently or in conjunction with the main power grid, microgrids enhance energy resilience, particularly during emergencies or grid disruptions. They enable communities to maintain a stable power supply, even in challenging circumstances, fostering self-sufficiency and reducing vulnerability to centralized energy systems.

In addition to rooftop solar panels and microgrids, community-based energy initiatives will thrive in 2100. Local communities will collaborate to establish renewable energy projects, such as wind farms, hydroelectric systems, or geothermal installations. These community-driven endeavors empower individuals to collectively invest in and benefit from clean energy generation. By pooling resources and expertise, communities can establish energy cooperatives, providing affordable and sustainable power to their members while fostering a sense of ownership and shared responsibility.

Decentralized energy generation offers numerous advantages. Firstly, it promotes energy resilience by diversifying energy sources and reducing the risk of widespread power outages. Localized energy systems are less susceptible to disruptions caused by extreme weather events or cyberattacks, ensuring a reliable supply of electricity.

Secondly, decentralized energy generation enhances energy equity. By enabling communities to produce their own power, even in remote areas, it reduces dependence on centralized power grids and improves energy access for underserved communities. This creates opportunities for economic development, empowers individuals to take control of their energy future, and reduces energy poverty.

Thirdly, decentralized energy generation contributes to the global transition toward a low-carbon economy. By relying on renewable energy sources, such as solar, wind, and hydro, communities can significantly reduce greenhouse gas emissions and combat climate change. This localized approach also minimizes energy transmission losses associated with long-distance power transportation.

However, the transition to decentralized energy generation requires supportive policies, technological advancements, and public engagement. Governments must create an enabling environment that encourages investment in clean technologies and supports the integration of decentralized energy systems into existing infrastructure. Collaboration between policymakers, energy providers, technology developers, and communities is essential to navigate regulatory challenges and ensure a smooth transition.

In conclusion, by 2100, decentralized energy generation will empower communities, enhance energy resilience, and promote energy equity. Rooftop solar panels, microgrids, and community-based energy initiatives will transform the way we produce and consume energy, fostering a sustainable and inclusive energy future. Let us embrace this vision, working together to build a decentralized energy landscape that benefits individuals, communities, and the planet as a whole.

· **Carbon Capture and Negative Emissions Technologies:**

In 2100, carbon capture and negative emissions technologies will play a crucial role in addressing historical carbon emissions. The chapter examines advancements in direct air capture, carbon sequestration, and utilization technologies. These technologies will help remove carbon dioxide from the atmosphere, mitigate the impacts of past emissions, and work in tandem with renewable energy to achieve carbon neutrality.

In the year 2100, these technologies will be instrumental in addressing historical carbon emissions, mitigating climate change, and creating a more sustainable world for future generations.

The chapter I will share with you explores the advancements in carbon capture and negative emissions technologies and their potential to reshape our approach to carbon reduction.

In 2100, carbon capture and negative emissions technologies will provide us with powerful tools to remove carbon dioxide from the atmosphere and combat the effects of climate change. These technologies encompass various approaches, including direct air capture, carbon sequestration, and carbon utilization.

Direct air capture technology involves capturing carbon dioxide directly from the ambient air using specialized systems. These systems utilize sorbents or solvents to selectively bind with carbon dioxide molecules, effectively removing them from the atmosphere. The captured carbon dioxide can then be stored underground or utilized in other industrial processes.

Carbon sequestration is another important aspect of these technologies. It involves capturing carbon dioxide emissions from power plants, industrial facilities, or other large sources and permanently storing them underground in geological formations, such as depleted oil and gas reservoirs or saline aquifers. This prevents the release of carbon dioxide into the atmosphere, reducing greenhouse gas emissions and helping to mitigate climate change.

Furthermore, carbon utilization technologies offer innovative ways to utilize captured carbon dioxide. Instead of simply storing it underground, captured carbon dioxide can be converted into useful products such as synthetic fuels, building materials, or chemical feedstocks. This approach not only reduces emissions but also creates economic opportunities and promotes the circular economy.

The development and widespread deployment of carbon capture and negative emissions technologies are essential for several reasons. First and foremost, these technologies allow us to address historical carbon emissions that have already accumulated in the atmosphere. By removing carbon dioxide from the air, we can mitigate the impacts of past emissions and work towards restoring a more stable climate.

Secondly, carbon capture and negative emissions technologies complement the transition to renewable energy sources. While renewable energy plays a crucial role in reducing future carbon emissions, these technologies offer a solution for sectors where complete decarbonization is challenging, such as heavy industry, aviation, or long-distance transportation. By capturing and storing or reusing carbon dioxide emissions from these sectors, we can achieve carbon neutrality and accelerate our progress towards a sustainable future.

However, the adoption of carbon capture and negative emissions technologies faces certain challenges. Technological advancements and cost reductions are necessary to make these technologies more economically viable and scalable. Collaborative efforts between governments, industries, and research institutions are crucial to drive innovation, enhance efficiency, and lower the costs associated with these technologies.

Moreover, policies and incentives are needed to encourage the deployment of carbon capture and negative emissions technologies. Governments can implement carbon pricing mechanisms, provide research and development funding, and establish regulatory frameworks that promote the development and deployment of these technologies on a larger scale. Public support and awareness are also vital in generating the necessary momentum to embrace and invest in these innovative solutions.

In conclusion, by 2100, carbon capture and negative emissions technologies will be powerful tools in our fight against climate change. These technologies, including direct air capture, carbon sequestration, and carbon utilization, will enable us to remove carbon dioxide from the atmosphere, mitigate historical emissions, and work alongside renewable energy to achieve carbon neutrality. Let us embrace these technologies, collaborate, and invest in their development and deployment to build a sustainable and resilient future for generations to come.

· **Socioeconomic and Geopolitical Implications:**

The energy revolution and clean technologies will have far-reaching socioeconomic and geopolitical implications. The chapter explores the economic opportunities, job creation potential, and the shift in global energy dynamics. It addresses the need for just transition policies, the importance of international cooperation, and the potential for clean energy to foster sustainable development and alleviate energy poverty.

In 2100, the energy revolution and clean technologies will have transformed the global energy landscape. The advancements in renewable energy, energy storage, electrification, sustainable buildings, and carbon capture will drive the transition to a sustainable and low-carbon future. By embracing these clean technologies, societies can achieve climate goals, foster economic prosperity, improve public health, and ensure a sustainable future for generations to come.

IX

Human Enhancement and Transhumanism

19

Augmenting the Human Body and Mind

The year 2100 presents a world where advancements in technology and scientific understanding have unlocked the potential to augment the human body and mind. This chapter delves into the ethical, social, and technological dimensions of human augmentation in 2100, exploring the opportunities, challenges, and implications of enhancing human capabilities.

- **Neural Interfaces and Cognitive Enhancement:**

In 2100, neural interfaces will enable direct communication between the human brain and digital devices, revolutionizing cognitive capabilities. The chapter examines the advancements in neuroprosthetics, brain-computer interfaces, and cognitive enhancement techniques, including memory augmentation, information processing speed, and enhanced learning abilities.

- **Biomechanical Enhancements and Physical Performance:**

Advancements in biomechanical technologies will augment human physical abilities in 2100. The chapter explores the development of exoskeletons, prosthetic limbs, and bioengineered tissues that enhance strength, endurance, and mobility. These technologies will enable individuals to surpass their natural physical limitations and improve overall quality of life.

In the year 2100, these technologies will revolutionize the way we interact with our bodies, pushing the boundaries of what is possible and enhancing the human experience.

The chapter I will share with you explores the fascinating developments in biomechanical technologies, including exoskeletons, prosthetic limbs, and bioengineered tissues, that will augment our strength, endurance, and mobility.

In 2100, these biomechanical enhancements will empower individuals to surpass their natural physical limitations and unlock new levels of performance. Let's delve into some of these exciting technologies.

Firstly, exoskeletons will play a pivotal role in enhancing human physical capabilities. These external robotic structures are designed to support and augment the movements of the wearer, providing additional strength and endurance. Exoskeletons can assist individuals in performing physically demanding tasks, whether it be in industrial settings, sports, or healthcare. By reducing fatigue and increasing strength, exoskeletons will enhance productivity, improve safety, and enable individuals to accomplish tasks that were once deemed impossible.

Secondly, the development of advanced prosthetic limbs will transform the lives of individuals with limb loss or limb impairments. In 2100, prosthetic limbs will not only replicate the appearance of natural limbs but will also provide enhanced functionality and sensory feedback. Neuroprosthetics, which establish direct connections between the prosthetic limb and the user's nervous system, will enable more intuitive control and restore a sense of touch and proprioception. These advancements will empower individuals with limb differences, enabling them to engage in a wide range of activities and participate fully in society.

Additionally, bioengineered tissues will contribute to the enhancement of physical performance. Scientists are exploring the development of engineered tissues that can replace damaged or aging body parts, such as cartilage, tendons, or muscles. These bioengineered tissues have the potential to restore function, improve mobility, and alleviate pain. By seamlessly integrating with the human body, these advancements will enhance overall physical performance and quality of life.

However, with these incredible advancements come important ethical considerations. Ensuring equitable access to these technologies is crucial, as they have the potential to exacerbate existing disparities. Efforts must be made to make these enhancements accessible and affordable to all, regardless of socioeconomic background. Additionally, ethical guidelines and regulations should be established to ensure the responsible use of these technologies, maintaining respect for human dignity, and protecting against potential abuses.

In conclusion, in 2100, biomechanical enhancements will propel human physical performance to new heights. Exoskeletons, prosthetic limbs, and bioengineered tissues will enable individuals to surpass their natural physical limitations, enhancing strength, endurance, and mobility. While these advancements offer incredible possibilities, it is vital that we approach them with careful consideration of ethics and accessibility. Let us embrace these technologies responsibly, ensuring that they contribute to a more inclusive and empowered future for all.

· **Sensory Augmentation and Perception Expansion:**

In 2100, sensory augmentation technologies will expand the limits of human perception. The chapter examines advancements in bionic eyes, enhanced hearing devices, and sensory neural interfaces that enable individuals to perceive a broader spectrum of stimuli. Augmented senses will transform experiences, enhance communication, and enable individuals to interact with their environment in unprecedented ways.

In the year 2100, these technologies will push the boundaries of human perception, allowing us to experience the world in ways we could only dream of before.

The chapter I will share with you explores the exciting developments in sensory augmentation technologies, including bionic eyes, enhanced hearing devices, and sensory neural interfaces. These innovations will enable individuals to expand their senses, perceive a broader spectrum of stimuli, and interact with their environment in unprecedented ways.

Imagine a world where individuals with visual impairments can regain their sight through bionic eyes. In 2100, these advanced visual prosthetics will not only restore vision but also enhance it. With the ability to see a broader range of colors, perceive finer details, and even have built-in zoom capabilities, bionic eyes will revolutionize the way we experience the visual world. From admiring the intricate beauty of nature to navigating complex urban environments, these advancements will empower individuals to fully engage with the visual realm.

Similarly, enhanced hearing devices will transform the way we perceive sound. In 2100, individuals with hearing impairments will have access to advanced hearing aids or cochlear implants that go beyond restoring basic auditory capabilities. These devices will allow users to hear a wider range of frequencies, detect subtle nuances in sounds, and even filter out unwanted noise. The world of music, conversation, and the sounds of nature will become richer and more vibrant, offering a whole new level of auditory experience.

Furthermore, sensory neural interfaces will enable direct connections between the human brain and digital devices, expanding our perception beyond traditional senses. These interfaces can translate digital information into sensory stimuli, allowing individuals to perceive and interact with virtual or augmented reality environments in a more immersive way. Imagine being able to experience virtual worlds with all your senses, truly blurring the line between the physical and digital realms.

However, as we explore the extraordinary possibilities of sensory augmentation, it is important to consider the ethical implications. Privacy, consent, and the potential for sensory overload must be carefully addressed. Additionally, equitable access to these technologies is paramount, ensuring that they are available to all individuals, regardless of their background or socioeconomic status.

In conclusion, in 2100, sensory augmentation technologies will revolutionize human perception and interaction with the world. Bionic eyes, enhanced hearing devices, and sensory neural interfaces will expand our senses, enabling us to experience a broader spectrum of stimuli and engage with our environment in unprecedented ways. As we embrace these remarkable advancements, let us do so responsibly, considering the ethical implications and ensuring accessibility for all.

· **Genetic Engineering and Biological Enhancements:**

The ability to modify the human genome will open doors to biological enhancements in 2100. The chapter explores the ethical considerations surrounding genetic engineering for traits such as intelligence, longevity, disease resistance, and physical appearance. The implications of genetic enhancements on equality, human diversity, and social dynamics will be examined.

· **Ethical Considerations and Regulation:**

The augmentation of the human body and mind raises profound ethical questions. The chapter addresses the importance of ensuring equitable access to enhancements, preventing societal divisions, and safeguarding human dignity. It explores the need for regulatory frameworks, guidelines, and public discourse to navigate the ethical complexities of human augmentation responsibly.

· **Psychological and Societal Implications:**

Human augmentation in 2100 will have significant psychological and societal implications. The chapter examines the impact on personal identity, self-perception, and social interactions. It explores the potential for societal stratification, discrimination, and the need for inclusive approaches to ensure that human augmentation benefits all members of society.

In the year 2100, advancements in human augmentation technologies will present us with exciting possibilities, but they also raise important questions about personal identity, self-perception, and social interactions.

The chapter I will share with you delves into the psychological implications of human augmentation. As individuals enhance their physical and cognitive abilities, questions about personal identity and self-perception will inevitably arise. How will these technological enhancements shape our sense of self? Will they redefine what it means to be human? These are complex questions that require careful exploration and consideration.

While human augmentation has the potential to empower individuals and improve quality of life, it also raises concerns about societal implications. The chapter examines the possibility of societal stratification, where access to augmentation technologies may create a divide between the augmented and non-augmented populations. It is essential that we work towards inclusive approaches, ensuring that the benefits of human augmentation are accessible to all members of society, regardless of their background or socioeconomic status.

Furthermore, we must address the ethical and moral challenges surrounding discrimination. In a world where individuals can enhance their physical and cognitive abilities, it becomes crucial to establish guidelines and regulations that prevent discrimination based on augmented or non-augmented status. Embracing diversity and promoting inclusivity will be vital in fostering a harmonious society that values and respects the inherent worth and dignity of every individual.

In addition to these societal considerations, we must also explore the potential impact on social interactions. As some individuals embrace human augmentation, it is essential to maintain empathy, understanding, and acceptance. Open dialogue and education will play a critical role in facilitating meaningful conversations and breaking down barriers that may arise between augmented and non-augmented individuals.

As we navigate the psychological and societal implications of human augmentation in 2100, we must approach these advancements with a responsible and ethical mindset. We must prioritize inclusivity, fairness, and the well-being of all members of society. By doing so, we can ensure that human augmentation technologies contribute to the betterment of humanity and promote a more equitable and compassionate world.

In conclusion, the psychological and societal implications of human augmentation in 2100 are vast and profound. We must carefully consider questions of personal identity, address societal stratification, combat discrimination, and foster inclusive social interactions. By embracing these advancements with a responsible and ethical approach, we can harness the potential of human augmentation to create a future that benefits all of humanity.

· **Human-AI Integration and Ethical Boundaries:**

As human augmentation intersects with artificial intelligence, questions of ethics and control arise. The chapter explores the ethical boundaries of human-AI integration, including issues of privacy, autonomy, and the potential for AI-mediated decision-making. It addresses the importance of maintaining human agency and ensuring that technology serves human interests rather than dictating them.

The augmentation of the human body and mind in 2100 offers remarkable possibilities for enhancing human capabilities and improving quality of life. However, it also poses complex ethical, social, and regulatory challenges. By navigating these challenges responsibly, society can embrace human augmentation in a way that respects individual autonomy, ensures equitable access, promotes human well-being, and upholds fundamental values. The careful consideration of ethical implications will be vital in shaping a future where human augmentation contributes positively to the advancement of humanity as a whole.

20

Ethical Boundaries of Transhumanism

The year 2100 presents a world where transhumanism, the philosophy that advocates for using technology to enhance human capabilities, has become a reality. This chapter explores the ethical boundaries of transhumanism in 2100, examining the complex ethical considerations and challenges that arise from pushing the limits of human enhancement.

Transhumanism is a philosophy that advocates for the use of technology to enhance human capabilities, pushing the boundaries of what it means to be human. In this chapter, we delve into the ethical considerations and challenges that arise in this brave new world of human enhancement.

The advent of transhumanism raises profound ethical questions about the limits of human enhancement. As technology progresses and allows us to enhance our physical, cognitive, and even emotional capacities, we must carefully examine the boundaries of these enhancements. What are the potential risks and unintended consequences? How do we balance the pursuit of enhancement with the preservation of human values and ethics?

One of the key ethical considerations of transhumanism in 2100 is the concept of autonomy. While individuals have the right to make choices about their own bodies and lives, the pursuit of enhancement may have far-reaching implications. It is important to ensure that individuals are making informed decisions, free from coercion or societal pressure. Respecting individual autonomy and ensuring that choices related to human enhancement

224

are truly voluntary will be paramount.

Equity and access to enhancement technologies are also significant ethical challenges. As advancements in human enhancement become available, we must strive for fairness and equality. It is essential to prevent the creation of a divided society where only a privileged few have access to these transformative technologies. Ensuring equal access to enhancement options will be crucial in fostering a just and inclusive society.

Furthermore, we must consider the potential consequences of transhumanism on the definition of human identity and the essence of being human. As we enhance our capabilities through technology, how does this impact our sense of self? How do we define what it means to be human in a world where technological enhancements blur the boundaries between biology and machinery? These philosophical questions require careful contemplation and dialogue.

Alongside these ethical considerations, we must address the potential risks and consequences of human enhancement technologies. Safeguarding against unintended consequences, such as unforeseen health risks or long-term implications, becomes crucial. Rigorous research, testing, and regulations are essential to mitigate potential harms and ensure the responsible development and deployment of enhancement technologies.

In navigating the ethical boundaries of transhumanism in 2100, collaboration among scientists, policymakers, ethicists, and society as a whole will be vital. Engaging in open and inclusive discussions, considering diverse perspectives, and maintaining a strong ethical framework will guide us in making informed decisions about the responsible use of human enhancement technologies.

In conclusion, the year 2100 promises a world where transhumanism has become a reality, pushing the boundaries of human enhancement. As we embark on this transformative journey, we must navigate complex ethical considerations. Respecting autonomy, ensuring equity, contemplating the essence of human identity, and mitigating risks are all essential aspects of ethical decision-making in the realm of transhumanism.

By embracing these ethical challenges, we can shape a future that harnesses the benefits of human enhancement while upholding our shared values and principles. Let us engage in meaningful conversations, foster collaboration, and navigate the ethical boundaries of transhumanism in a manner that reflects our collective aspirations for a better and more inclusive world.

1. Defining Transhumanism: The chapter begins by defining transhumanism and its core principles, highlighting the pursuit of physical, cognitive, and emotional enhancements through technology. It explores the vision of transhumanists to transcend human limitations and the potential benefits and risks associated with such transformations.

2. Autonomy and Informed Consent: Ethical considerations of transhumanism in 2100 revolve around the principles of autonomy and informed consent. The chapter examines the importance of individuals making informed decisions about the extent and nature of their enhancements. It delves into the challenges of ensuring genuine autonomy and consent in the face of societal pressures, commercial interests, and potential coercive influences.

3. Equity and Access: Transhumanism in 2100 raises concerns about equity and access to enhancements. The chapter explores the potential for a technological divide, exacerbating social and economic inequalities. It discusses the ethical imperative of ensuring equitable access to enhancements, addressing issues of affordability, distribution, and ensuring that enhancements do not further marginalize disadvantaged groups.

4. Human Dignity and Identity: Transhumanism challenges the concepts of human dignity and identity. The chapter examines the ethical implications of altering the fundamental characteristics that define our humanity, such as our physical appearance, cognitive abilities, and emotional experiences. It explores the need to respect and preserve human dignity while pursuing enhancements.

5. Safety and Long-Term Consequences: The chapter delves into the ethical obligation to prioritize safety in the development and imple-

mentation of transhuman technologies. It examines the potential risks and long-term consequences of enhancements, including unintended side effects, psychological impacts, and unknown health risks. The importance of rigorous testing, regulation, and ongoing monitoring is emphasized.

6. Impact on Society and Social Structures: Transhumanism in 2100 will have a profound impact on society and its existing structures. The chapter explores the ethical implications of these transformations, including questions of social cohesion, cultural diversity, and the potential for creating new forms of discrimination. It discusses the importance of engaging in inclusive and democratic deliberations to shape the societal impact of transhumanism.

7. Ethical Limits and Responsibilities: The chapter addresses the question of ethical limits in transhumanism. It explores the need to define boundaries and establish guidelines to prevent ethical overreach and unintended consequences. It discusses the importance of maintaining a holistic perspective, considering the broader societal, environmental, and intergenerational implications of transhuman enhancements.

Transhumanism in 2100 offers unprecedented possibilities for human enhancement but presents significant ethical challenges. By navigating the ethical boundaries of transhumanism with careful consideration, society can embrace advancements while preserving human values, promoting equity, and safeguarding individual autonomy and dignity. Responsible decision-making, robust ethical frameworks, and inclusive public discourse will be crucial in shaping a future where transhumanism contributes to the betterment of humanity without compromising our fundamental ethical principles.

X

Reflections on the Journey

21

Epilogue: Looking Back, Looking Forward

As we reach the end of this book, it is time to reflect on the journey we have taken together and look back at the remarkable advancements and ethical considerations that have shaped our future. The year 2100 is not only a culmination of human achievements but also a stepping stone to a future filled with endless possibilities.

Throughout the preceding chapters, we have explored various technological frontiers, from AI and automation to renewable energy, genetic engineering, and human augmentation. We have examined the ethical implications of these advancements, delving into the complexities of balancing progress with responsibility, ensuring equity, and safeguarding our values as a society.

Looking back, we can appreciate the transformative power of technology in shaping our world. We have witnessed the rise of renewable energy, marking a turning point in our fight against climate change. The proliferation of AI and automation has revolutionized industries, changing the way we work and live. Genetic engineering has unlocked new possibilities for human health and well-being, while also raising important ethical considerations. And the concept of transhumanism has challenged our perceptions of what it means to be human.

Yet, as we celebrate these achievements, we must also acknowledge the lessons learned and the challenges we faced along the way. We have seen how technology can amplify existing inequalities, disrupt job markets, and encroach upon personal privacy. We have grappled with questions of responsibility, accountability, and the potential unintended consequences of our actions.

In looking forward, we must carry these lessons with us as we continue to shape the future. It is our collective responsibility to use technology ethically, ensuring that it serves the betterment of humanity as a whole. We must strive for equity, inclusivity, and the preservation of our shared values. As we embark on new frontiers, we must approach them with a mindful and ethical mindset, considering the impact of our actions on future generations.

The future holds both excitement and uncertainty. It is a canvas awaiting our collective imagination and efforts. It is up to us to chart a course that honors our values, respects human dignity, and safeguards the planet we call home. By embracing the wisdom gained from our past and the knowledge at our disposal, we have the opportunity to forge a future that is not only technologically advanced but also ethically sound.

As we close the final chapter of this book, let us carry the lessons learned, the ethical frameworks developed, and the conversations sparked within its pages. Let us continue to explore the frontiers of knowledge, always mindful of the ethical considerations that accompany our progress. Together, we can shape a future that is not only bright but also grounded in our shared humanity.

Thank you for joining me on this journey of exploration and reflection. May we look back with pride, and look forward with hope.

9 798395 235640